Gunnar Hedlund

This is Riding

Dressage, Jumping, Eventing in Words and Pictures

Translated by Sigrid Young

Foreword by
Elwyn Hartley Edwards

Harrap  London

Foreword

Gunnar Hedlund stresses at the beginning of this book that in order to learn to ride it is necessary to go to an experienced instructor. Very rightly, he also emphasizes that riding is a difficult thing to do properly — something which is not always admitted, or even understood, by many of those who inflict themselves on the long-suffering horse.

Riding, and an appreciation of the difficulties involved, is of course learnt in the riding school; but the study of books is of almost equal importance to the serious horseman.

Books provide a base of theoretical reference which complements and can indeed clarify even further the practical instruction given in the school.

Of course, it all depends on the quality of the book, which must be as good or even better than the standard of instruction. This, I believe, is just such a book, and its combination of succinct text and brilliant illustration places it amongst the best half-dozen to have appeared in my lifetime.

ELWYN HARTLEY EDWARDS
Editor, *Riding* Magazine

London, January 1981

First published in Great Britain 1981
by GEORGE G. HARRAP & CO. LTD
182 High Holborn, London WC1V 7AX

First published by Albert Bonniers Förlag, Stockholm 1978 *under the title* Detta är ridning

© *Gunnar Hedlund* 1978

English translation © *George G. Harrap & Co. Ltd* 1981

D.L.B. 11130-1981
Printer Industria Gráfica sa   Provenza, 388   Barcelona

ISBN 0 245-53766-X

Printed in Spain

Contents

Pictures and words help us to learn
    about riding 4
The muscles of the horse 6
The skeleton of the horse 7
The mind of the horse 8
The reflexes of the horse 10
Factors affecting performance 12
The capability of the horse and the
    objective of the rider 14
The foal 16
The foal in the mare's company 18
The yearling and two-year-old 20
Lungeing and work over cavalletti 22
The inexperienced horse and what it
    can do 24
Basic riding instruction — revision 26
The various ridden figures 29
Lateral work and turns on the
    forehand 30
The walk 32
The trot 32
The canter 34
Transitions 36
Rein-back 37
The straightening of the horse 38
Balance 40
The half-halt 41
The halt 42
Halt — Salute 43

Dressage

Ballet dancer — Dressage horse 46
Equipment 47
Dressage at shows 48
The trot 50
Extended trot 52
The canter 54
Changes of direction 60
Pirouette 62
Leg-yielding and lateral work 64
Exercises in lateral work 66
Piaffe 72
Passage 76

Jumping

Controlled explosion — the
    show-jumper 80
Equipment for the show-jumper 82
The technique of the show-jumper 84
Loose-jumping 86
Cavalletti work 88
Gymnastics 89
Training of the jumper on the flat 90
Canter with increased collection 92
The way to jump 94
The way to the jump 98

During the approach 102
Just before the take-off 104
The take-off, first phase 106
The take-off, second phase 108
Moment of suspension over the
    obstacle 110
The landing 112
Various fences 114
High jumps 116
Spreads 120
Combinations 122

Eventing

The horse at events — a disciplined
    devil 126
The dressage test 128
Show-jumping 129
Fitness training 130
Gallop work 131
Work to build up the horse 132
Timing 133
Roads and tracks 134
On the steeplechase course 135
Cross-country 136
Typical cross-country fences 138

Index 142

Pictures and words help us to learn about riding

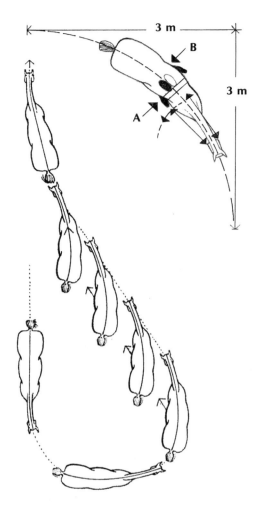

Riding is a game, a hobby, a pleasure. As with any other game that is worth while, it has to be taken seriously to gain full benefit and pleasure.

There is no doubt that riding is difficult, which adds to its interest and fascination. It is practically impossible to become perfect, but it is always possible to improve. The art does not only give the rider pleasure, but provides a challenge to try to establish a harmonious physical relationship with the horse. The more the rider advances, the greater the challenge.

It is essential to have a teacher when one is learning to ride, but a well-thought-out book with instructive pictures can be a valuable support to the teacher's lessons, and is always on hand for reference. This is the aim of the present book.

It is suitable for the beginner as well as the advanced rider and anyone who is interested in improving their riding. Watch, feel with your body and then try to understand what the teacher is aiming at.

Riding is not something that the rider does in isolation; it is a joint effort of two living creatures, the rider and the horse. In order for them to function as one, it is necessary for them to work together with as little friction as possible. To reach this goal the rider has to work smoothly to obtain the obedience and attention of the horse.

This book aims to help the interested rider to improve himself. It tries to show through word and picture that horse and rider can and should be as one.

To really understand his horse the rider must know about anatomy and its relationship to movement. That is why there are diagrams of the muscles and skeleton, and why the reflexes, the mind and the factors affecting movement and performance are discussed.

It is important that the foal should develop under the watchful eye of its mother, and that a trust of humans be fostered to create the right conditions for it to grow up into a good horse.

It is necessary for the rider to have a basic knowledge of the following to pro-

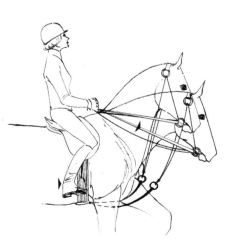

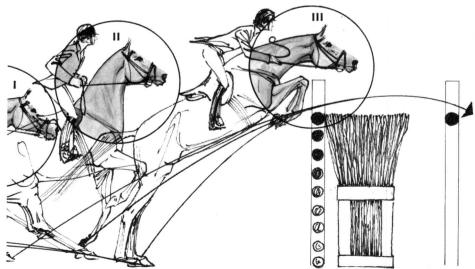

gress and improve: to be able to lunge, to work the horse over cavalletti and to possess a knowledge of the aids and how they relate to each other. When one studies the paces of the horse, the sideways movements and the horse's behaviour, it becomes obvious how important that knowledge is.

This book shows step by step, in progressive pictures and drawings, how horse and rider can work together in the development of the former's muscles, and in making it supple, so that it can carry its own weight as well as its rider's in a balanced way.

The next step is to find out the direction in which horse and rider want to develop, which depends somewhat on the ability and talent of both, for it could be towards Dressage, Show-jumping or Eventing.

Each lesson of the advanced training is usually concentrated on two facing pages. When dealing with the jumping, each phase is separately explained in detail, with a small explanatory diagram on each page. The special equipment

that is needed for competitions, whether Dressage, Show-jumping or Eventing, is fully explained at the beginning of each discipline. Three of the best-known Swedish competition riders contribute to the sections concerned with their particular disciplines: Ulla Håkansson (Dressage), Jana Wannius (Show-jumping) and Janne Jönsson (Eventing).

Gunnar Hedlund has drawn the pictures in this book to show as clearly and in as great a detail as possible the 'Sequences of Movement'. He was able to do this because he is both an experienced teacher and a talented artist. The reader can therefore improve his knowledge by examining the clearly drawn pictures, which will give him some idea as to whether he is on the right lines or not.

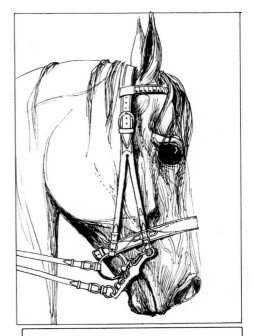

Explanation of signs

= Aids and direction

= Passive hand

= Weight-displacement is towards the dark oval

≫ = Flexion of joints

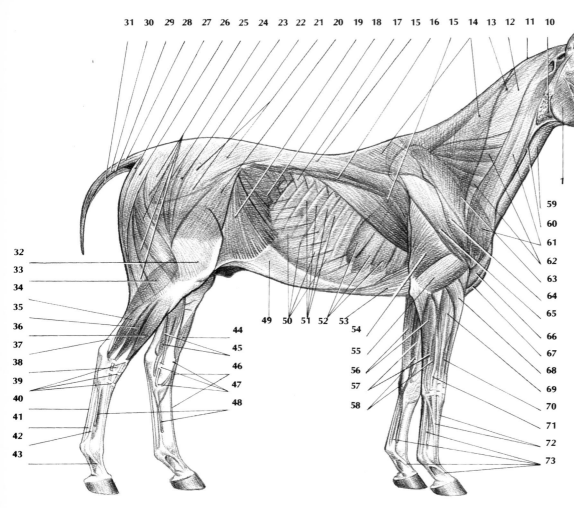

The muscles of the horse

1 Masseter (Outer Jaw Muscle)
2 Zygomaticus
3 Depressor of the Lower Lip
4 Orbicularis Oris
5 Chin
6 Levator (Lifter) of Upper Lip and Wing of Nostril
7 Lateral Dilator of Nostril
8 Buccinator
9 Temporal
10 Parotid Salivary Gland
11 Nuchal Ligament (Ligamentum Nuchae)
12 Splenius
13 Complexus
14 Trapezius
15 Latissimus Dorsi
16 Longissimus Dorsi
17 Dorsal Serrate (Caudal Part)
18 Flank Region
19 Internal Oblique Abdominal
20 Tensor of Fascia of the Thigh (Tensor Fasciae Latae)
21 Gluteal Fascia over Hind Region
22 Superficial Gluteal
23 Hip Joint
24 Trochanter of Femur
25 Biceps Femoris
26 Semitendinosus
27 Semimembranosus
28 Levator (Lifting) Muscles of the Tail
29 Lateral (Sideways Pulling) Muscles of the Tail
30 Intertransverse Muscles of the Tail
31 Depressor Muscles of the Tail
32 Vastus
33 Gastrocnemius
34 Digital Flexor Muscles
35 Lateral Digital Extensor
36 Long Digital Extensor
37 Achilles Tendon
38 Hock Joint
39 Annular Ligaments (Retinacula) around tendons
40 Superficial Digital Flexor
41 Deep Digital Flexor
42 Suspensory Ligament
43 Branch of Suspensory Ligament to Extensor Tendon
44 Cranial Tibial
45 Deep Digital Flexors
46 Tendon of Long Digital Extensor
47 Annular Ligaments (Retinacula) around tendons
48 Splint Bones
49 Tendinous Sheets of the Abdominal Muscles
50 External Oblique Abdominal
51 Intercostal Muscles
52 Ventral Serrate (Serratus Ventralis) (Thoracic Part)
53 Pectoral (Caudal Part)
54 Triceps (Long Part)
55 Triceps (Lateral Part)
56 Flexor Muscles of Carpal Joint
57 Superficial Digital Flexor
58 Deep Digital Flexor
59 Sterno-Cephalic
60 Jugular Vein
61 Brachiocephalic
62 Ventral Serrate (Neck Part)
63 Supraspinatus
64 Infraspinatus
65 Deltoid
66 Shoulder Joint
67 Pectoral (Cranial Part)
68 Radial Carpal Extensor (Extensor Carpi Radialis)
69 Common Digital Extensor
70 Oblique Carpal Extensor
71 Lateral Digital Extensor
72 Extensor Muscle Tendons
73 Suspensory Ligament

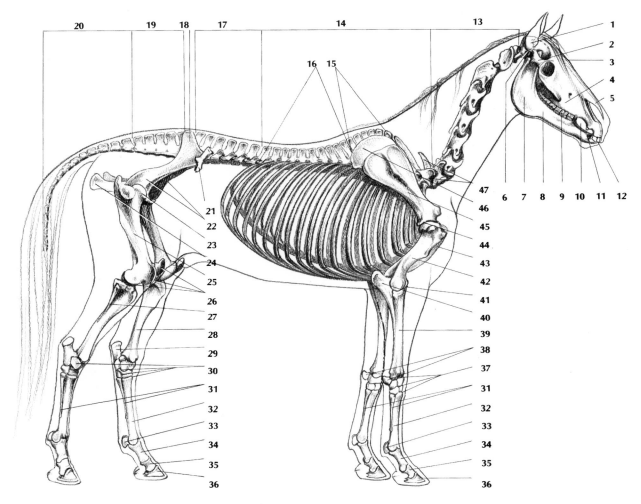

Dr R. N. Smith of Bristol University kindly supervised the preparation
of the key to these two diagrams for the English-language edition.

The skeleton of the horse

1 Occipital Bone
2 Zygomatic Arch
3 Frontal Bone
4 Maxilla (Upper Jaw)
5 Nasal Bone
6 Opening of Ear Canal
7 Ramus of Mandible (Lower Jaw)
8 Body of Mandible (Lower Jaw)
9 Cheek Teeth (Molars and Pre-Molars)
10 Diastema (Tooth-free space of Upper and Lower Jaws)
11 Canine Tooth (Tush)
12 Incisor Teeth

13 Cervical (Neck) Vertebrae. A: Atlas B: Axis
14 Thoracic Vertebrae
15 The 8 'True' Ribs, attaching to Sternum
16 The 10 'False' Ribs, joined to one another by cartilage
17 Lumbar Vertebrae (5 or 6)
18 Tuber Sacrale (Sacral Tuber) (Point of Croup)
19 Sacrum, usually 5 vertebrae fused together
20 Caudal (Tail) Vertebrae (16-18)
21 Tuber Coxae (Point of Hip)
22 Pelvis

23 Hip Joint
24 Tuber Ischii (Ischial Tuber) (Point of Buttock)
25 Femur (Thigh Bone)
26 Patella (Knee Cap) and Stifle Joint
27 Fibula
28 Tibia
29 Calcaneus forming Point of Hock
30 Hock Joint
31 Small Metacarpals (Forelimb), Small Metatarsals (Hindlimb) (Splint Bones)
32 Large Metacarpal (Forelimb) Large Metatarsal (Hindlimb) (Cannon)
33 Sesamoids at Fetlock Joint
34 Proximal Phalanx (Long

Pastern, Os Suffraginis)
35 Middle Phalanx (Short Pastern, Os Coronae)
36 Distal Phalanx (Coffin Bone, Pedal Bone, Os Pedis)
37 Carpal Joint (Carpus, Knee)
38 Accessory Carpal Bone (Pisiform)
39 Radius
40 Olecranon (Point of Elbow)
41 Elbow Joint
42 Humerus (Upper Arm)
43 Sternum (Breast Bone)
44 Shoulder Joint
45 Scapula (Shoulder Blade)
46 Scapula Cartilage (Cartilage of Prolongation)
47 First Thoracic Vertebra with its strong spinous process

The mind of the horse

The brain — a computer

The brain of the horse should be envisaged as a computer which receives and stores information. There are also various traits which can be inherited and may be inbred in certain breeds. One stallion may be noted as a sire of jumpers, while another may produce good dressage horses, etc.

In the central nervous system of the foal there is already a built-in pattern which, for example, dictates its paces. Therefore, the new-born foal has relatively well-developed paces. The horse is basically a herd animal, and the foal has to be able to follow its mother and the herd from the moment it is born. During its growth the computer system works out the changes in the body in relation to the bones, muscles and limbs. At the same time the experience with its mother, other youngsters and human beings adds to its development. Its movements become more co-ordinated and established.

The central nervous system sends out impulses to the various muscles. At the same time it stores information with the help of the senses. For example, the condition of the ground, the shape of obstacles, the presence of a steep slope or a ditch are registered with the help of the visionary sense, while the aids of the rider are registered by the horse feeling the pressures made by legs and hands, etc. The central nervous system is connected with the sense of balance, and is also responsible for activating the muscles that regulate the horse's movements.

The sense of balance

This mainly controls the position of the body, change of direction and change of pace. The sense of balance is responsible for the production of involuntary reflexes which preserve the equilibrium of the body. Especially important are the reflexes that influence the position of the head with the help of the neck muscles.

The sense of touch

A 'muscle memory' is built up by the horse through routine and experience, which is then put into a long-term store. It is not often that a horse repeats a mistake. For instance, if a horse hits a fence its nervous system registers pain, and it learns to avoid this by tucking up the legs to avoid hitting the pole again. If the pole is not hit there is no sensation of pain. The nervous system is used by the rider to communicate with his horse through the aids given by the legs and hands. At the beginning of the work with the horse the aids should be given clearly and strongly. Later on they can be reduced to only light pressures.

The skin of the horse has many small nerve centres which, when touched, send the information to the central nerve centre, where it is interpreted. The answer from the computer to a certain sequence of aids given by body, hand and leg may be, for example, 'left canter'. A change of pressure indicates an increase or reduction in speed. Long-sustained pressure tires a horse's nerve system by dulling the impulses which are a reaction to the pressure. That is why the aids of the rider should not be given for too long at a time, and this is one reason why the saddle should spread the weight of the rider over as large a bearing surface as possible.

The sense of hearing

The horse's sense of hearing is far superior to that of human beings. The ability to hear sounds of various strengths is almost unbelievable, and the rider should use this to his utmost advantage.

A single clicking of the tongue by the rider can encourage the horse to jump with more enthusiasm and snap. A soft voice and patting by the rider will quieten a horse. A sharper tone of voice will be taken as an admonishment, while the word 'Good' spoken encouragingly will be understood as being praise for something well done.

In most cases a horse can be trained to be more obedient and easier to handle if, when it is a foal, words like 'Good' and 'Halt' are used.

When a horse has learned to interpret the various intonations of the voice no other aids will be necessary. For example, if the rider says 'Halt' in a firm voice the horse should still be mounted.

Vision

The scientists have not yet completed their research into the vision of the horse. One cannot compare its eyesight with that of humans, especially as the eye is in a completely different position.

It is not possible to know how fully the horse can differentiate between colours, although experiments have proved that it is easier for it to see yellow and green than blue and red. It has also been established that when there are two jumps of the same height but in different colours, the horse finds one more difficult than the other.

The contrast between the colours of the jump and the surroundings is of importance. It is possible, for example, that the horse finds it more difficult to jump a blue obstacle than a red one. The assumption, moreover, is that the horse cannot focus as a camera would to obtain a sharp image: it finds it difficult to judge distances in the way that a human would. It has to change the position of its head to look at a certain object, and make small movements with its eye to get the object into focus. When the horse moves or the position of the head alters, it changes the angle at which both eyes look at an object.

2. When the horse looks at an object on the ground some distance away the light-rays are retained in the retina (**A**). The object is registered and reproduced. The closer the horse gets to the object, the higher the picture has to fall in the

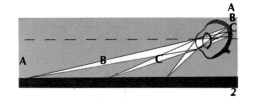

retina (**B** and **C**), so that it can be clearly seen (i.e. reproduced). The broken line is the optical axis.

4. When the horse looks straight ahead with its head slightly raised it can see the green area with both eyes (about 60°). It can see the yellow and blue area with one eye, and the black area not at all.

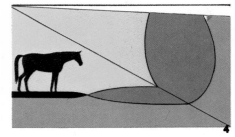

The lower picture gives the view from above of the areas the horse can see with either one or both eyes. The white line represents the black of the previous picture.

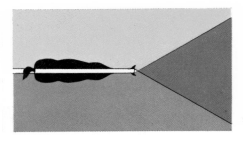

1. The nearer the horse gets to an obstacle the better it can judge the width of it. The horse learns to use its perception to judge distances.

3. When the object is on a higher level the horse's vision must be raised. **B — B** corresponds with B in the previous picture. The horse seems to be able to judge the height of various obstacles relatively well, but not so well, for example, the width of a parallel. In spite of this it manages these fences well, probably because of their solid appearance, which induces it to make a greater effort.

Horses probably make mistakes over some fences because they cannot judge the width and height properly. To be able to look up the horse has to raise its head.

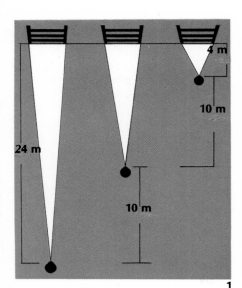

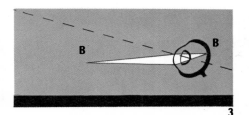

The reflexes

A reflex is the reaction of the central nervous system to a stimulus. The impulses pass through the central nervous system, but are not consciously registered.

Standing, walking, jumping — in fact, all movements, including those of the inner organs (such as those concerned with digestion) — are activated by reflexes. The so-called patella (kneecap) reflex is the one which moves the leg when the tendon is hit below the knee. This is an example of the unconscious, inbred reflexes which can be motivated at any time, and which are very difficult — in fact, almost impossible — to stop. Conscious and conditioned reflexes are easier to check. They can also disappear when not used. For instance, the human mouth is inclined to water when we look at a succulent titbit. This is a conditioned reflex which is caused by the optical stimulant. When the horse moves sideways through the pressure of the rider's leg, or starts cantering when the rider increases the pressure on the saddle, these can be regarded as conditioned reflexes.

Dressage consists largely of the horse being conditioned to certain reflexes. A great number of reflexes are unconditioned, such as the neck and balance reflexes.

The central nervous system functions as a very complicated signal box where changes are recorded and impulses are carried along to activate the various muscle groups of the body. There is also a built-in control mechanism which registers how strong the conscious impulses are — e.g., if and how the horse will react, and how slowly or quickly.

A 'programme' can be temporarily blocked, and then the horse will not react at all. For instance, a horse having lost concentration may not listen to leg or rein aids. A rider with feeling or an experienced teacher can see and feel whether a horse is receptive or not. It is very difficult to explain this to a nervous or tense student.

Neck and balance reflexes

When the horse moves its neck up and down or sideways it creates further impulses which in turn move various muscle groups.

When a horse raises his head and neck in the approach to a jump (**A**) the fore-legs stretch out instinctively and the hind-legs bend.

Immediately before landing (**B**) the same reflexes are released. The fore-legs are stretched, the hind-legs bent and the head and neck raised.

When the horse lowers its neck and strides out the hind-legs stretch and the fore-legs bend. This is clearly seen in the second phase of the jump (**C**).

Every rider who jumps must know these reflexes, and understand that since they are essential to the horse's performance he must not interfere with them.

When a rider sits in a way which hampers and interferes with these unconscious reflexes he stops the horse from jumping correctly and effectively, causing it to hollow the back instead of rounding it. The rider can make use of the horse's natural sense of balance when it uses its head and back to balance itself at speed.

The horse can turn regardless of the way in which the neck is bent. It turns its head and neck away from the way it is going for better balance, and to obtain a better footing.

One can compare the reflex movements of the horse with those of the slalom skier who turns away from the direction he is going to get a better

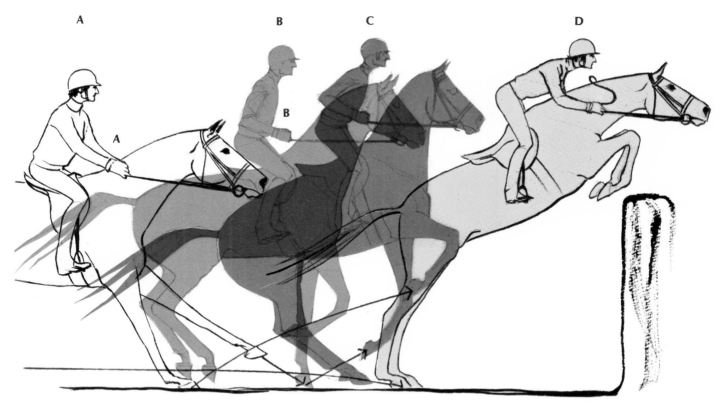

*When the height of the jump is increased the horse uses its stomach muscles rather as a pole-vaulter uses his arms to push himself forward and up. This is only for a very short moment, and is an instinctive reflex produced by the size of the fence and the need to make an extra effort. When the head of the horse comes into a more horizontal position the fore-legs will bend at the same time as the hind-legs stretch. The rider who is in harmony with his horse can influence it to make a greater effort in the take-off. At the moment of take-off (**A**), when the fore-legs are stretched, the rider must react quickly and not interfere (**B**). When the fore-legs come off the ground (**C**) the pressure stretches the hind-legs (**D**). This way the rider can use the horse's natural reflexes (see also page 107).*

grip with his outer ski, while at the same time the inner ski, together with the inner shoulder and arm, aids his direction. Therefore, the horse should keep its 'false position' (i.e., the neck turned away from the movement) when moving round a bend at speed — on a show-jumping course, for instance. When going fast across country the horse will keep its balance better when it is allowed to position itself. It sometimes even changes leg when galloping if it feels it is necessary, and when negotiating a corner.

Horse with the 'wrong bend' when cantering with the right leg leading round a bend.

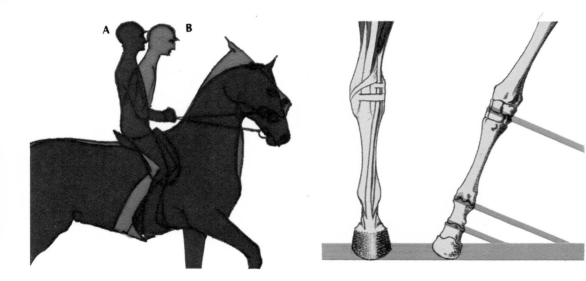

Factors affecting performance

Many things can interfere with the horse's movement and affect the overall performance. These are some of the factors involved:

- The rider
- Condition of the ground
- The hoof and shoeing
- The mechanism of the hoof
- Pain

The rider
The weight of the rider on the horse's back has a disturbing influence, especially when he is not properly balanced. This has the effect of a badly packed rucksack on a man's back, and upsets the horse's equilibrium. The rider's centre of gravity should correspond in all positions with the centre of gravity of the horse. Only then can a proper balance be achieved, and the aids correctly given. It gives the horse the opportunity to carry out the rider's wishes.

The going
The horse's muscles and tendons can be strengthened by riding it over different types of ground. The rider should be in the position to judge whether or not the going is suitable for it, and whether it could cause damage. Very hard going can do a great deal of damage to the horse's muscles, and pull tendons, especially in the upper part of the hind-legs. The same applies to deep mud, where the horse's feet sink in, and it is difficult for it to pull them out. Even at shows there is frequently not enough attention paid to the condition of the ground. There are also very badly designed racetracks. It happens quite often that the riding-in area has a good covering of grass and is springy, while the arena where the competitions take place is hard, with only a covering of dry sand. It is quite obvious that this unsettles the horse, and does not always lead to the expected results.

The hoof and shoeing
Neglected feet and bad shoeing can be avoided. A good blacksmith can save the horse a lot of misery, and the rider worry. The hoof must be properly looked after, and the horse must be shod regularly every five to seven weeks.

If the hoof gets too long it changes the position of the foot, which can be damaging. The shoes must fit properly so that the horse does not strike one leg against another. If the horse has problem feet these can be corrected by the blacksmith.

The working of the foot
The foot mechanism of the horse is very complicated, and I will try to explain it as simply as possible.

The whole weight of the horse, approximately 400 to 500 kg (8-10 cwt) rests on the four feet. In trot the weight is carried alternately on each diagonal pair of legs, and in canter for a brief

The Hoof

A *Extensor Tendon*
B *Cannon Bone*
C *Suspensory ligament*
D *Deep flexor tendon*
E *Superficial Flexor tendon*
F *Sesamoid*
G *Fetlock*
H *Sesamoidian ligament*
I *Short pastern bone*
K *Navicular Bone*
L *Pedal Bone*
M *Plantar cushion*
N *Sole of hoof*
O *Frog*

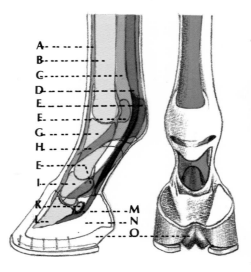

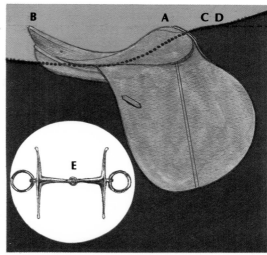

Middle: A side view of the hoof.
On the right: A properly shaped saddle. The saddle is in the proper position when the pommel and cantle (A and B) do not touch the horse. It must lie evenly on the horse's back so that the deepest point of the seat is in the centre and the pommel does not touch the wither. The saddle should be slightly behind the wither (C and D).
To avoid the horse's mouth getting sore, the snaffle shown in the inset picture is advisable (E).

moment on one foot alone. The weight is concentrated on the fetlock, and then on the pastern, which presses on the digital cushion and then the rest of the foot. The foot is elastic, within the confines of the wall, and changes shape when weight is applied. The various parts of the foot change in relation to each other. When there is pressure on the fetlock the pastern is pressed into the plantar cushion, causing the elastic sole of the foot and the frog to spread themselves and press the elastic cartilage sideways. This affects the heels of the foot which run into the frog.

The heels expand to about 10mm when the foot is not shod. They expand at the junction with the frog and then shrink again, mainly into the sole of the foot.

The foot mechanism works quite normally in healthy unshod horses. The shoes are nearly always at fault when there is trouble; therefore it is most important to have a good blacksmith who will take care and who understands the structure of the foot and the relationship

of the working parts.

The surface of the shoe which lies against the hoof must be flat and smooth. Nails are never put inside the white line which marks the division between the sensitive and insensitive laminae. The shoe must be sufficiently long (about 5mm) behind the bars and wide enough to ensure a full bearing surface for the wall of the foot.

Shoeing the horse is done to save the foot from being worn away too much. Sometimes too much pressure is put on a particular part of the leg or foot when studs are used. The angle of the bones in the foot may be changed as a result when the weight is not evenly distributed, and this can lead to pulled ligaments, inflammation of the joints and strained tendons.

Pain

Bruises and flesh wounds are usually noticed straight away and treated. Sprains are also easily detected, as the horse goes lame. Damage to the back and ligaments through excessive work

is, unfortunately, only discovered when it is too late, as such damage is usually gradual, and not very noticeable to begin with. Riding-school horses are especially prone to such damage; they are ridden by beginners who let them go with a hollow back and not on the bit when riding in a confined manège. When lameness is detected the horse is rested, but as soon as it starts work again the lameness will recur.

All horses can suffer from ill-fitting saddles, which because they cause discomfort can affect the performance adversely.

There is also the matter of the bit, which if it is of the loose-ring type can become so worn that sharp edges rub against the mouth. A bit with cheeks, or an eggbutt, can prevent this, and so can rubber shields, but the latter are not permissible in dressage competitions.

The capability of the horse and the objective of the rider

The ability and talents of the horse

Some ability is inherited. Certain mares and stallions produce good dressage horses while others produce good jumpers. Consistent and careful breeding can produce top-class horses. The English Thoroughbred and the American Standardbred trotter are examples of where selective breeding is used to produce the best. The horses used are those that have proved themselves on the racecourse, and this especially applies to the stallions. Modern breeders place as much importance on the ability of the mare as on that of the stallion. The line of mares that have proved themselves should not be subject to experiments. When breeding Thoroughbreds it might be desirable, as well as testing the horses used for breeding, to have statistics of their show results.

With the help of video and slow-motion photographs it would be possible to study the way a horse uses himself when jumping. In this way the breeders would be able to assess earlier the ability and potential of their young horses, and it would ensure that buying a young horse would not be such a risk. Good progeny which might not have been discovered otherwise could now be passed on to efficient riders who could make the best of them, and be successful in their chosen spheres. But inherited ability is not everything. There are event horses which get so keen on the cross-country course that the rider has difficulty in controlling them. Some such horses have been re-schooled by dressage riders and have made exceptionally good horses for dressage, as they are very forward-going and active. The reverse has happened occasionally when dressage horses who showed every likelihood of reaching the top were re-schooled to become jumpers. They applied themselves with great enthusiasm and exceptional ability. The good grounding, of course, had helped to discipline and balance them, but it had also bored them. But they had really enjoyed jumping, and gave of their best.

The objective of the rider

Every rider who wants to enter in competitions will of course choose the sphere to which he is most suited, and which he enjoys the most. If jumping is his main interest, he will mainly jump; the dressage enthusiast will ride his figures, and the keen event rider will gallop across country as though the devil were after him.

It is easy for the rider to forget that the dressage horse likes a jump now and then, the jumper a little dressage and the event horse an easy hack out. I am sure there are serious riders with good theoretical knowledge who consider the needs of their horses and give them the change they need now and then.

There must be harmony between the aim of the rider and the ability of the horse. If a rider wants to jump and the horse is better at dressage it is advisable for him to get another. Both horse and rider must have pleasure in their work together.

It happens frequently that the horse submits to such an extent that it is difficult for the rider to read the signs that say 'I am bored; can't we do something else?' The rider is so interested in getting on and achieving great things that he loses contact with his horse and its needs. He is then unable to understand its character.

A good rider has to be attentive and study his horse, to find out about its background and origin. He must try to find out its reflex reactions, and its reactions to his aids; in general, which side of the sport his horse is most suited to, and where it is most likely to achieve success. The horse is a willing creature, and it is up to the rider to give him every chance. The only way to gain greater knowledge and deeper insight is by sympathy. One of the best Swedish trainers of show-jumpers, Dag Nätterqvist, said:

A rider must have the same attitude to riding as a believer to his religion. He has to believe in riding in all its forms. He has to believe in the horse and has to try to do everything right all the time. To keep on studying the seat, the different styles, the actions of the horse, the origin, the performance, etc. Always ask the question "Why?" Why is it like this or like that? Examine and question again and again. Analyse. Read everything you can lay your hands on about horses and riders. It is absolutely necessary to understand the fundamental theories. To know the psychological as well as the physiological reactions, the possibilities, the weaknesses and strengths of the horse and the limits of its capabilities. You must know exactly what you want and what you are aiming at. *You must have a goal!*

There should be no preconceived idea when choosing a career for a horse. Looking at the bay horse on the left — his free shoulder movement suggests a good all-round horse, while the grey on the right seems to lend itself ideally to becoming a dressage horse and the one below has a good natural style of jumping. But the temperament plays a most important part. A jumper must not be too fiery, while a Thoroughbred-type horse with a great deal of energy and sensitivity is apt to be nervous, and not take kindly to the discipline of dressage.

The foal

A foal is able to walk, trot and canter only a few hours after being born. It moves rather awkwardly, but with an inborn grace, on legs that are too long in relation to its body. Rapidly, day by day, its ability to move safely over uneven ground increases; it seems to have 'eyes in its toes'. It rushes at full speed all over the place, and jumps ditches and other obstacles which even a fit person would treat with great respect. Its sense of balance is complete, and its suppleness enviable. It expresses the joy of freedom by leaping and bucking. It trots along with head and tail high, its trot almost like a 'passage'; as if to say 'Look at me – look what I can do.'

After suckling its eyelids get heavy, it lies down and is fast asleep in no time with the complete confidence that 'Mother will look after me'.

The horse in the service of mankind

Mankind likes to dominate all living creatures, and has been able to tame the horse and make it its willing servant owing to the horse's accommodating nature. We want to dominate the horse's life. We have considerable influence on its breeding and propagation, but our interference must stop at a certain point, such as letting nature take its course in the relationship of mare and foal. We must be extremely careful to create a sympathetic relationship be-tween man and foal. Ideally the foal must gain complete confidence in man from the moment it is born, and feel it can rely on him entirely.

To create in the horse the feeling of security man has to study its nature, and to build up a feeling of confidence which will lead to harmony. This is just what we are looking for – the close working together of the human under-standing and the finely developed instinct of the horse.

The senses of the horse are keenly developed. Its hearing is finely attuned to the nuances of the human voice. A quiet, soft voice can help to settle a startled horse and persuade it to come to you to seek shelter and security.

It is important that the mare has the qualities that are needed in the offspring. She is the one that looks after the foal's education. It is a great advantage for the foal to come into contact with man as early as possible so that it gets used to him. Such horses are later on easier to school, and have greater trust in their rider.

The steady and soft (as well as firm) hands of a clever and purposeful rider can make the horse give performances beyond expectation. But horses, like people, have their own idiosyncrasies. Are there really wicked horses? Hardly, for the horse reacts by instinct, not reason; it acts according to its instinct, but reacts to pain and outside influences. It also reacts to the mood of the person dealing with it. If a person is restless and tense, this is transmitted straight away to the horse; it will lose its confidence, and become unsettled. Its first instinctive reaction is to try to get away.

We must try to understand the horse by living as close to it as possible and observing its actions. The mare does the same when the foal returns to her after playing. Watch the horse, how it reacts to anything new, how it approaches carefully, investigates it, listens, sniffs at it, tenses, hesitates, prepares to run away if the unknown should appear dangerous.

The first experiences

The mare is the foal's first teacher. She guides it round the field, shows it the fence, the paths, the water where it can drink. She keeps it away from marshy ground and bogs. She encourages it to move about, to play, to trot, to canter, but only to the extent that it does not tire itself too much. She knows how much it is able to do without straining itself.

We know that children can be trained to greater achievements than seemed possible some time ago, but we know in addition what psychological and physiological effect that can have on these children. This does not apply to animals. The mare gives the impression of being the best mother imaginable. (The stallion has little to do with the foal.) She displays no vanity or possessiveness, only instinctive care of her foal.

The trainer and rider should adhere to the same rule. The rider must consider how much he can ask of his horse. Fitness and stage of education dictate what can be demanded.

The training of the foal's reflexes is important. A foal will follow its mother wherever she goes, and so learns the right reaction automatically.

In Mother's company

The foal should get used to wearing a head-collar as soon as possible after it is born. It will accept this as an established daily routine, as it will having its feet lifted to pick out the hoof. It should also become a habit for the foal to be led with the mare. The next step is to have the foal accompany the mare when she is ridden. It is good for the mare to be ridden daily for a short time while she is suckling; that is, if she had

been ridden and was in training before she foaled. The foal can then go with her. They can even go over a few small jumps of about half a metre together. There must be no pressure; this must be treated as fun, so that the foal gets used to some small obstacles, and uses its reflexes. One often sees it give a small buck after the jump – a sure sign that says 'This is fun.'

A half-hourly daily hack, consisting

mainly of walking, short trot periods and a half-minute canter, teaches the foal some discipline. It is not designed to develop its muscles.

The foal thinks: 'Mummy and man are going where I have never been before. I don't want to leave my mummy – I'll follow her.

'What strange things we come across – I wonder if they are dangerous. It seems not. Now Mummy stops and

It would be wise for those who handle foals and horses to realize at the start that the best way to train the foal is to take it along when you are riding the mare. Note that the mare is ridden in a mild cheek snaffle, which will not hurt its mouth, and a plain drop noseband.

starts grazing. The man gets off Mummy's back. I am allowed to go free. How lovely! So many new things. I skip about because it is all such fun. I am hungry and go and have a drink from Mummy. Ah, that is good. Now I see the man puts the rope on my head-collar again and gets on Mummy's back. Off we go – I wonder where? We canter. There is a pole and we jump over it, that was nice! I buck with pleasure. What is

it I can smell? The stable, the field. Can't we go faster? I want to get home to the stable or the field. Quick, Mummy, I am tired, I want to go to sleep.'

The head-collar is taken off, the saddle and bridle off the mare. A sleepy foal lifts its feet to have them checked, and the gate is closed after the mare and foal. The mare has a roll, gets up and grazes. A sleepy foal lies down. Its eyelides start drooping and get heavier

and heavier; it stretches out and goes to sleep.

Again another step has been taken to consolidate the trust between man and foal. A little more experience and knowledge have been added. What will become of the little horse? Watch it; study it carefully; you have to make the best of your horse without any false pride.

The yearling and two-year-old

The yearling

It is of great advantage to all horses to be turned out even in winter and in the snow so that they can use up their surplus energy. This applies especially to young horses. The yearling is undergoing the most rapid growth period of its life, and any 'training' has to be undertaken with great caution.

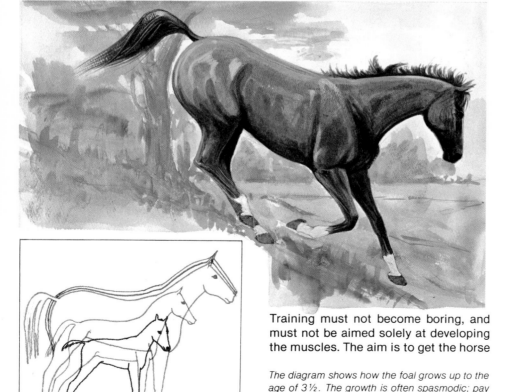

There has to be a warming-up period, first either by its being led for half an hour or by its being put on the lunge for twenty minutes. The training can start with approximately ten minutes' work over cavalletti, interchanged with simple jumps for about five minutes daily. Jumping, cavalletti, lungeing or being led should be interchanged day by day.

Training must not become boring, and must not be aimed solely at developing the muscles. The aim is to get the horse

The diagram shows how the foal grows up to the age of 3½. The growth is often spasmodic; pay special attention to the loins and the wither. It is beneficial to the foal if it is on somewhat hilly pastures when it is growing.

to practise its reflexes and to establish its reaction to the voice. The yearling will learn through constant repetition to judge distances, to trot and canter, to know when to take off and how much effort is needed to get over an obstacle. Some horses, of course, take longer to learn than others. Some have difficulty in judging the right point to take off. Such horses must be allowed to make mistakes. Always make sure to train the horse on both reins, as it might otherwise lead to crookedness later on. The distances between cavalletti and jumps should be 20 per cent shorter for a yearling and 10 per cent for a two-year-old than for a fully grown horse.

The process of growing

The rapid growth of the yearling can quite likely cause it pain at times. The legs are especially susceptible, and are apt to hurt.

Training as well as feeding has to be increased very slowly. Even when growth is unusually rapid, feeding must be commensurate. Too much work can cause a fusion of vertebrae in the back. The latter would then become stiff, and its use for general riding and jumping correspondingly restricted.

The two-year-old

Sadly, many promising two-year-olds are spoilt every year, as too much is demanded of them before they are psychologically and physically ready. The racetrack and trotting track would surely benefit if the commercial aspect could be ignored and the youngsters were not rushed, and had more time to

develop. The Thoroughbred is reared for early maturity, but the half-bred horse is definitely not ready to be trained as a two-year-old. It should be left to develop quietly without asking for perfection. Always remember to reward and praise the horse.

The work with cavalletti should be carried on, and slowly made more difficult. The loose-jumping should be varied, and the obstacles raised, but not too high. The two-year-old can be familiarized with all sorts of jumps and combinations. Steady work over these will settle the horse, and get its jumping technique established, though care should be taken to see that it does not lose its pleasure in jumping, and enjoying life.

When it reaches the age of 2 to 2½ it should get used to the bit and be worked with the snaffle. It is best to use a thick snaffle with cheeks so that it does not move about in the mouth. Make sure the bridle fits properly, and that the noseband is high enough not to obstruct the breathing. It should be possible to put two fingers between noseband and nose when the former is properly fitted.

At this age long reining can also be started. A roller with rings can be used, and the reins put through the rings. These have a similar action to that of the reins later on. Long reining is an excellent way of teaching the horse circles, turns and sideways movements and at the same time keeping it relaxed. Make good use of the voice, and this also will be preparation for a closer contact between horse and rider later on.

There are all sorts of possibilities of schooling the horse by long reining, and subsequently, if desired, a sulky or trap can be used.

When the horse reaches the age of 2½ to 3 it can be taught to accept the saddle. From now on it can be asked for more obedience and stricter work. The exercises remain much as before, but can be used to build up muscles gradually. The horse can be led on long hacks over difficult ground, and the training over cavalletti and jumps increased in order to strengthen it, and prepare it to carry the rider. To get the horse used to the rider it is best for him to hang over the saddle and gradually get on and off.

On the lunge

When starting to lunge a horse it is a good idea to have an assistant. The lunge-line is fastened on to the inside ring of the head-collar. In this way it can act in restraining or leading. The instructor starts by leading the horse on to a circle on the right rein. His elbow is at its shoulder, and thereby he keeps it on the circle. When the horse goes quietly on the circle the instructor moves slowly away towards his assistant, who is holding the lunge-line and whip, and takes over from him. The instructor then carefully raises the whip and points it towards the horse's hip. If the horse falls into the circle he points the whip at its shoulder to keep it out. The whip is held in the left hand for the right rein and right hand for the left rein, with the lunge-line in the opposite hand.

Cavesson

The yearling is usually lunged in a head-collar with the lunge-line attached to the rings on either side, as he is used to this and it is comfortable for him. Later on, when the work on the lunge has progressed, a cavesson with swivelling nose and side-rings should be used. This is firmer, and rests more securely on the horse's nose. It takes a little longer to fit a cavesson, but it pays off, since it is more comfortable. The noseband must not slip down, lest it obstruct the horse's breathing. Be careful to fit the cavesson in such a way that the side-pieces do not slip forward and interfere with the eyes. The inside of the

cavesson should be soft and clean, and a sheepskin padding could be put under its noseband to stop chafing. A properly adjusted cavesson should lie comfortably over the usual bridle and snaffle-bit.

The whip

The whip takes practice to make it effective, and to use it correctly. The horse respects the whip. It should therefore be used quietly, and in such a way that the horse does not shy away from it. It is not raw strength that makes a whip effective but the acquired knack of twisting it and causing it to crack (see G). With practice one can get a whip to crack from all angles. The horse has to be taught respect for the whip, and should not be frightened of it.

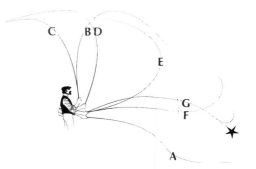

Lungeing and work over cavalletti

The most important thing when lungeing is to keep a contact between the hand and the horse's mouth (see previous chapter on cavesson). The chambon is a great help, as it never acts backward; it acts only through a slight pressure on the neck. The fitting of it is shown in the picture below. The horse reacts to the chambon by lowering its head and stretching its neck forward and initially downward. By encouraging steady forward movement the horse will move rhythmically, with lowered hocks and active back (see picture below).

The small picture shows how the instructor should stand in relation to the horse and the position of the whip, which is pointing to the shoulder, to stop the horse falling into the circle. After some time lungeing, if carried out correctly, will develop the animal's loins, which are the weakest point.

Lungeing should be done on a circle of 14-metre diameter. The cavalletti are spread out in fanlike fashion. The distances should be 1·30m for the trot, and for the canter 3·50m. A two-year-old should not jump more than three to four times over three cavalletti.

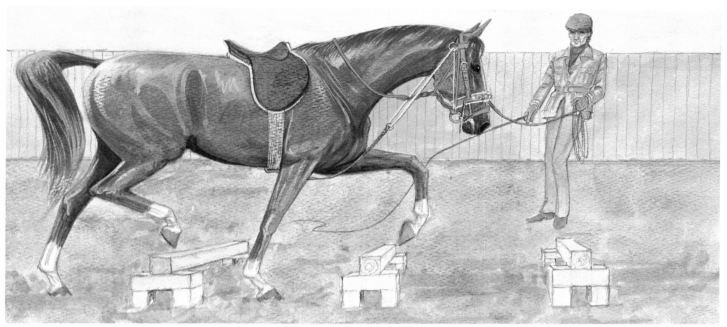

Above and left opposite: Start off by lungeing the horse on a volte (6m circle) inside the big circle. When it has settled gradually increase the circle and let it jump over the cavalletti, which have been placed fan-fashion (see picture).

Below: Cavalletti can be combined with jumps. Put a pole with one end on top of the jump, the other resting on the ground. In this way the lunge-line can slip over it, and does not get tangled up with the jump. Do this in trot and canter, but when cantering take off the chambon and/or side-reins.

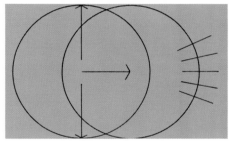

Always have someone to help you when first mounting a horse.

Go out hacking in the woods as soon as possible to test its reaction and widen its horizon.

The inexperienced horse and what it can do

It is quite a different matter to sit on a completely green horse, which has just been pulled out of a field, compared to one which one has handled since it was a foal. The former is not at all used to stables or a stable routine, and neither has it had much contact with human beings.

It will have problems to adjust to the new routine, and not too much should be asked of it. When starting to ride such a horse one will realize that the time spent with the foal and youngster has not been wasted. Now is the time to prepare the horse for work in all the different phases, dressage, jumping and eventing.

It is an exciting day when one mounts a young horse for the first time. There is some tension in the air — but is that necessary? No, not at all, because you have already leant over the horse many times, and even sat on it without a saddle. Get it used to the saddle by putting it on, and letting the animal stand thus in the stable for some time. Then lead it about a bit so that it gets used to the feel of the saddle when moving.

You should always have help when you get up for the first time. Get your helper to lead the horse while you are sitting on it. Your assistant could also help you on the lunge. Ride a small circle, and then let the horse trot so that you can see how it reacts to your weight in the trot. Gradually the helper can let go of it. Now you are alone with your horse. You are riding it. It recognizes your voice, your smell, your coaxing hand. It knows that it is you who instilled confidence in it during its early training. A click with the tongue will make it move on, a restraining hand will make it halt. Sit on the left hip-bone; the horse will move to the left; it wants you

Ride the young horse over undulating ground and jump ditches to improve its balance and initiative.

Always ride forward and change weight when changing direction.

in the middle of its back. Well done!

Assert some pressure with the lower leg, click at the same time, and ease the reins. The horse trots on. It works! Do rising trot straight away to ease the horse's back. Trot lightly and in rhythm. Talk to your horse and watch its ears, which tell you a lot. The horse is listening to you. 'Whoa' — sit down slowly and gently. Pat it and praise it. It has been good, and done what you asked of it. You gave it every chance to obey your commands, and it did.

Hacking out

When the horse has been worked for 10 to 15 minutes in an indoor school or outside arena, take it out for a hack — just walking and some rising trot. Make it go forward with leg-aids and an easy rein. When trotting there should be a light contact, not a slack rein. Let your hands rest near the withers but do not fix them: just ease either one or the other rein when changing direction.

Pay special attention to correct rising and sitting when trotting. The seat is in the saddle when the off fore touches the ground. When changing direction always change the diagonal; also when trotting straight for a long time, so that not too much weight is put on the one leg.

A consistent urging with the lower leg and clicking will in time help the horse to become active. The muscles of the loins will begin to build up; the horse gets used to the rider's weight and gains strength.

Try not to interfere, and let it jump over low and inviting logs.

Basic riding instruction–revision

It is not possible for anyone to be a perfect rider. There always comes the time when one asks oneself 'Why is the horse doing this? What am I doing wrong?' That is the time when one has to go back to the beginning and check one's aids and the horse's reaction. A revision now and then of the basic principles of riding can be very useful.

The dressage seat

The rider sits deep in the saddle. The seat is in the middle of the vertical line which passes through the centre of gravity of the horse and the rider's shoulders lead the forward movement. The hips and heel should be practically in line, the back straight and the upper arm hanging relaxed, while the lower arm and hands should be in line with the reins to the horse's mouth. The pelvis is pushed slightly forward, the knees lie on the saddle, with the knee itself pointing forward. The lower leg should be slightly back to allow it to come into contact with the horse.

The chief thing is for the rider to sit comfortably and relaxed, and to follow the horse's movements with a supple back.

The jumping seat

This seat is used when jumping fences, as well as cavalletti and cross-country. It will take the weight off the horse's back and make it easier for the animal to use its head and neck and to balance itself. The rider does not sit in the saddle; the stirrup leathers should be shortened three to four holes, but not made too short so that the rider cannot sit into the saddle if necessary. Thigh and knee are on the saddle, and the lower leg behind the girth, the heel well down and toes turned out slightly and the stirrup brought home. The hips should be pushed forward a little without lowering the back. The upper body is pushed forward to a greater degree than when doing rising trot (*see page 33*). The shoulders are in a relaxed position, and the lower arm and hands are in line with the reins to the horse's mouth. It is important that the rider does not sit down heavily in the saddle and snatch at the horse's mouth, as this would upset its balance and rhythm. By being supple and pliable in hip, knee and wrist, and leaning forward, the rider can stay balanced in all the horse's movements.

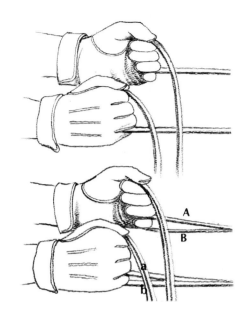

Position of the reins

The snaffle reins run through a loose fist (*see picture above*), between the little and third finger and over the index finger, and are held in place by the thumb. The position of the hand is such that the thumb is always on top. The back of the hand should be in line with the lower arm. Hold the hands close to each other, and about the width of a hand above the wither.

The double bridle is made up of the curb bit and bridoon. The left (**A**) and the right (**a**) reins, connected to the curb, run between the little and the third finger. The left, connected to the bridoon (snaffle) (**B**) and the right rein (**b**), go under the little finger. Both reins join over the index finger, the thumb preventing them from slipping. The pressure of the snaffle-rein can be increased by closing the hand tightly and turning it slightly towards the body, with the little finger leading.

The aids of the rider

These are the leg, the hand, the seat, voice, spurs and whip. None of the aids are used on their own — always in conjunction with each other. It is therefore very important that they are used properly, as the horse can easily get confused and upset (*diagram in the middle of the paragraph*). The main forward driving

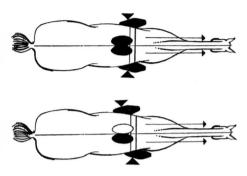

aid is the leg which presses against the side of the horse. Seat, upper and lower leg, knee and heel all act together, sometimes strengthened by the spur. The lower leg can lie on or behind the girth; in exceptional circumstances in front of the girth. The pressure must be reduced as soon as the horse responds to the aids, as a constant pressure will deaden its reaction. Spurs are only used when they are really necessary. The whip and clicking of the tongue also aid the leg.

Restraining aids are mainly given with the reins, though these must be combined with pressure of the leg on the horse and a deep seat — that is to say, restraining aids must be supported by forward aids, and indeed preceded by them. There should be several give and

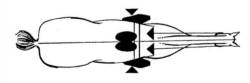

take movements, never a steady restraining pull. When the horse obeys the pressure of the hand the latter should be released, the horse being thus rewarded.

The rider can either ease the reins by turning his hand so that the little fingers point towards the horse's mouth or to a greater degree by moving his hands forward. It does not pay to jerk the horse's mouth if it does not react to the aids; it will only resist and get a hard mouth. It is best to try to get response by giving and taking of the rein with a light hand (*see rein-back, page 37*).

The reins are kept in contact with the horse's neck on either side, and then used to guide it. The head should be nearly vertical, with the ears parallel, while the upper part of the neck is only bent so far that the rider can see the nostril and eyebrow (*see diagrams*).

The rein is usually only taken away from the neck when riding unschooled horses. It is used, for example, when the rider wants the horse to make a turn on

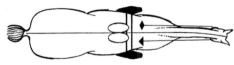

the haunches on the left rein. When riding a schooled horse the rein remains against the neck. When taking the rein away from the neck of the horse, it goes towards the hip of the rider and not the waist. When the reins remain against the neck the weight is shifted slightly to the left and the right leg is behind the girth.

Seat aids The rider uses his weight to shift the centre of gravity from one seat-bone to the other. The seat should be firm in the saddle, and the inside hip pushed forward and the knee lowered. The rider must not drop his inside shoulder and bend sideways, as that would move the weight to the outside. The weight reinforces the leg and rein aids, especially when making turns on the forehand and haunches, leg-yielding and transitions to the canter.

The riding out of corners

The rider turns his horse to the inside, approximately three metres before a

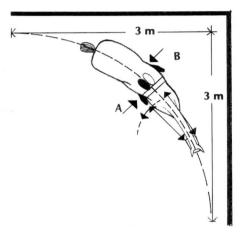

corner. When riding an unschooled horse the right rein could be taken away from the neck for easier guidance. The horse moves steadily forward between the rider's legs. The inside leg of the rider is placed on the girth, and motivates the inner hind-leg of the horse. The rider puts more weight on the inside seat-bone, pushes the inside hip forward and lowers the knee. The horse must not be allowed to let its hind-quarters swing out (**B**) — the rider's outside leg, which is placed behind the girth, should control this. The outside rein steadies the horse's neck so that it does not get too much of an inside bend. The horse and rider should be straight again shortly after the corner — approximately three metres.

The correctly bent horse on a circle. To show more clearly how the rider should sit in a circle, he has been lifted out of the saddle. His vertical line corresponds with that of the horse. The outside leg is slightly back. Compare this sketch with the one showing the horse from above. The weight is on the inside seat-bone. The outside hand is passive while the inner hand guides, keeps contact, and keeps the horse on the circle.

Riding of circles

It is difficult to ride a true circle without a properly positioned horse. Prepare the horse with a half-halt — i.e., push with legs on to a momentarily restraining hand. Position it with the inside rein in the direction you want it to go, and keep both legs on. The horse must not lose its rhythm. The aids are the same as those used when riding through a corner (*see page 27*). Put weight on the inside and look in the direction you are going.

It often happens that when the circle is half-way completed the horse drops its outside shoulder and loses its bend. It can also happen that the horse resists and goes crookedly. Now we go back to the moment when horse and rider leave the track to start the circle. The outside leg and correct rein has to be used so that the circle finishes at the same point where it began. The rider has to be careful to distribute his weight properly. Use even pressure with both seat-bones, ease the inner rein and keep the horse straight with the outer one. Both legs are on the horse, driving him forward.

Think forward and the horse will also think forward — that is how it is achieved. The rider drives with his seat and legs. The horse's hocks bend and the hind-legs come under the body, the hindquarters are lowered resulting in a raising of the neck. The rider gives and takes with the reins until the horse relaxes his lower jaw and becomes light in front, due to the increased engagement of the hind-legs under the body.

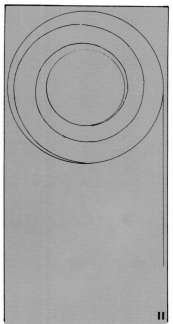
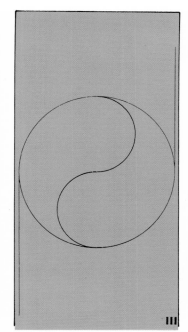
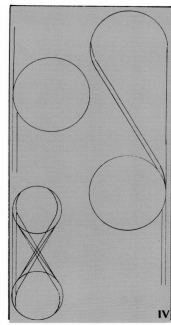

The various ridden figures

To supple one's horse various figures can be ridden in the manège. Change of direction and different bends all help to supple and balance the horse, strengthen the muscles and make it pay attention.

Above: Figures ridden in Sweden
Below left: Figures ridden in Germany, which are also used to a great extent in England

A *The horse is correctly bent from neck to tail to go through a corner*
B *The horse's neck is bent away from the direction it is going in the leg-yield*

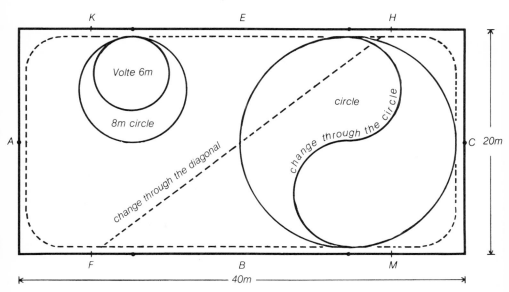

Figures ridden in the riding school.

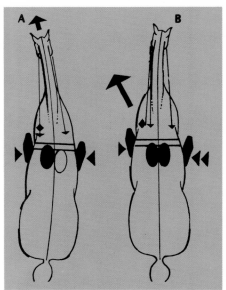

Lateral work and turns on the forehand

Leg-yielding and lateral movements can be practised with the aid of long reins which go through the rings on the roller. The instructor stays behind the horse and does not use a whip. The advantage of this method is that it is easier for the horse to move forward.

Suppleness of the horse can be achieved through lateral work. It is best to start teaching it from the ground. The instructor stands on the inside of the horse — that is, on the side to which it is turning. In this position it is between the instructor and the wall of the school, and cannot escape the whip. The instructor rests the hand holding the reins on the wither and clicks his tongue to encourage the horse. The horse is held on the bit with its neck bent away from the direction of the movement. The whip is held in the other hand, and touches the horse slightly behind the saddle to encourage it. The horse should be on two tracks in walk and trot with an almost straight body. It must be encouraged to go forward all the time, and must not overtrack more than half a metre. As soon as the horse is used to the whip it is good to move away from the track to keep it going forward.

Turn on the forehand to the right with the left (inner) leg back and the left rein in contact. The inside fore-leg is on the ground, and becomes the centre of the half-circle. The inner hind-leg crosses over, and is in front of the outside hind-leg. Both lower legs are on the horse so that it does not creep backward. The reins prevent the horse from moving forward, but it must not step backward. The outside leg makes it perform the turn step by step. The outside rein is eased if the horse does not use its fore-leg, and prevents a crooked neck developing.

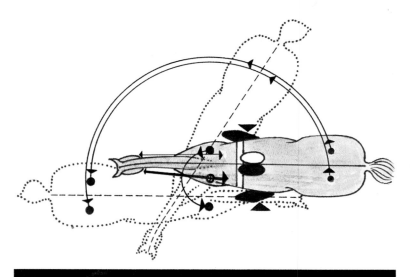

The horse is learning the two track movements and leg-yielding in hand with a snaffle-bridle. The horse must be held straight, and not be allowed to get away from the whip. The horse's neck is bent to the right, in the opposite direction to the movement, and steps with its inside legs over and in front of the outside ones.

Leg-yielding with rider

Start this exercise with a half-halt. The rider should be sitting in the middle of the saddle, the horse's head turned slightly away from the direction it is asked to go. At the same time the pressure of the inner leg should be increased, which encourages the horse to go sideways. The leg is just behind the girth, and the whip if needed is behind the leg. The outside leg which lies on the girth encourages the horse to go forward, but it also regulates the angle and stops it from evading action of the inner leg asking for the lateral movement. The outside rein is in contact and leads the movement. These aids should work together in rhythm with the horse's movements. The inside, sideways driving leg and inside rein should be active when the inside hind-leg is lifted.

At the beginning it is enough for the horse to do only one or two sideways steps, and the number of steps can then be slowly increased. When it has learn-ed to accept and understand the aids the movement can be done at the trot. In this pace it is easier to keep the impul-sion. One of the easiest ways to practise leg-yielding is on the way home from a hack, when the horse is warm and wants to get home. Be careful! The horse must never be forced to do lateral movements without proper preparation. Don't get cross if a movement is not successful, but praise the horse and ride straight at once if one has been well performed.

Turns on the forehand

These are used to make the horse supple and as a preparation for the rein-back.

This exercise is started from the halt. It is very important, as it is in leg-yielding, to bend the horse slightly to the inside and keep the impulsion going. The turn of the forehand is done mainly at 180°, as shown in the picture. Several turns, one after the other, can be made to soften the neck and lower jaw. As soon as the horse gives, make it go forward with slightly stronger driving aids. In the working trot the horse should move for-ward on the bit. The turns should be practised on both reins so that they get equally well established.

The rider should sit straight and relaxed without lowering the hip or pushing the outside leg forward. Head and eyes are turned towards the point where the movement finishes.

A *Walk on a long rein. Easy seat. The horse's head moving in rhythm with the steps.*
B *Collected walk. Seat and hands are moving with the horse. The head is raised.*

The walk

The walk is a pace of four-time. The foot-falls are as follows: left hind, left front, right hind, right front. When the horse steps correctly it is easy to hear the four footfalls.

Pacing and jogging

If the horse is pacing it moves both right or left legs at the same time, and swings forward, using alternate lateral pairs. It is very difficult and takes a long time to cure a horse of pacing. It has to go back to a slow walk on a long rein, and come back to the rhythm of the walk in four-time.

Jogging is a transition from walk to trot. The horse starts a diagonal footfall, but the hind-leg is obstructed by the fore-leg on the same side, so cannot take a proper stride. Not to be left behind, the horse increases the number of steps. If a horse is not sufficiently relaxed and not on the bit it will not walk

out properly but take short strides and not overtrack. Highly strung horses often do this, but it can also be caused by the rider giving too strong aids without easing the reins.

The correct walk

The correct walk is quiet, and covers the ground. The walk shows the rhythmic movement of the horse's head and neck. With each footfall of the fore-legs the head is lowered, and swings forward. The rider must not interfere with this swinging movement, especially if the horse goes against the bit. This movement is a natural reflex action, and must not be hindered or the horse could start pacing. If a young horse is asked for collection in the walk too early, this can also result in pacing.

It is very important that the rider has contact with the horse's mouth, and moves in rhythm with its movements,

and has a sympathetic hand which follows the horse's mouth. A good rider who moves with his horse looks as though he had a hinge in his back.

The trot

The trot is a movement in two-time. The legs move alternately in diagonal foot-fall. Right hind-leg, left fore-leg. Left

A Rising trot when doing working trot. Sit in the saddle when outside fore-leg and inside hind-leg touch the ground (see sketch of hoofprints). The picture shows how high the rider lifts himself off the saddle, and the angle of the upper body. The hands have a steady contact with the reins, and the lower leg urges the horse forward. B Sitting trot. Supple waist and back. Upright seat. Quiet hand. The lower leg pushes the hocks under the horse and on to the bit.

hind-leg, right fore-leg. The hind-legs have the more important function; they push from the ground forward. Immediately after each thrust with the hind-leg it should be possible to see all four legs suspended off the ground. The balancing movements of the head and neck stop almost completely: they are not needed, as the weight distribution stays the same. In the true trot only two hoof-beats are heard, as the diagonal legs meet the ground at the same time. The trot is not true when it is four-time. It is pacing or ambling. This is nearly always caused by the horse being tense, and loosening-up work and two-track exercises should help. According to the circumstances, the trot is ridden either rising **A** or sitting **B**.

The rising trot

The rising trot is used to make it easier for horse and rider. The rider rises at each second stride and follows the rhythm of the horse. It is usually the movement of the horse which activates the rising in the saddle. The drawing shows how high the rider rises and how much he leans forward.

A The position of the leg remains the same. The horse's outline must not change in the rising trot. It must stay on the bit. Each time the rider sits down the pressure of the leg is increased, and in this way a driving aid is given every other stride. To use the leg in between these strides upsets the rhythm. The daily exercise should always start with the rising trot. The rider can rest the middle-finger joints against the wither.

The hand is steadier, and the rein-aids more definite.

Change of diagonal in the rising trot

The rule is that the rider follows the outside fore-leg. He sits when the outside shoulder reaches the farthest point and at the same time the inner hind-leg touches the ground (*see hoofprints below left*). When changing the rein, the diagonal should be changed too. The rider misses one beat.

Sitting trot

The rider should sit straight and as deep in the saddle as possible, with a supple back (**B**). The stirrup irons should only carry the weight of the foot. The legs should have a constant light contact with the horse. The rider should not keep his balance by hanging on with knee or lower leg.

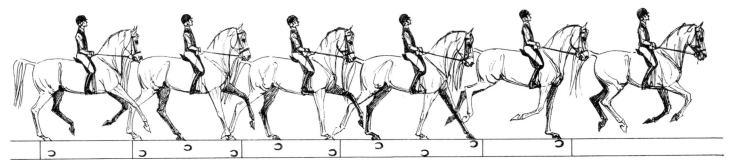

Footfalls in canter. The horse pushes alternatively with one, two or three legs.

The canter

The canter is a more comfortable pace for the rider than the trot. It is easier to follow the movements of the horse. The canter is a jump-like movement with a moment of suspension; this varies from horse to horse. One differentiates between left and right canter. The leading leg is always on the inside — i.e., left fore leading on canter on the left rein and vice versa.

The footfalls in the canter can have three variations (*see diagram below*). **A** is the usual footfall in the working canter. **B** is collected canter, **C** mostly in gallop. **A** and **C** is canter in four-time — you can hear four footfalls. **B** is in three-time — you can hear three footfalls.

The horse is said to be on the wrong leg if it strikes off with the opposite leg to the one the rider has asked for — for example, leading with the left leg on the right rein. The above is called counter-canter when the rider asks for it (*see page 56*). It is always wrong if the horse is disunited (*see page 54*).

In the canter the rider should follow the horse's movements with a firm but supple seat (*see picture above*), sitting deep in the saddle with the pelvis pushed slightly forward. The knee and instep are soft and springy so that the rider does not come out of the saddle. When the horse is cantering quietly the hands should be still, with just a slight contact with the horse's mouth.

Strike-off to canter

It is easiest for the horse to strike off into canter, from the trot, in the corner after the short side. First give a half-halt so that the horse does not rush into the canter. Position the horse slightly to the inside, shift your weight a little by lowering the knee on the inside. The outside lower leg lies just behind the girth. Pressure with the inside lower leg asks for canter.

The horse has already learned to canter as a two-year-old. When riding a young horse it is quite all right for the rider to use his voice and whip to reinforce his other aids. The horse starts off by transferring the centre of gravity to the hindquarters, thereby taking the weight of the fore-legs, and it is now able to canter. When the horse starts to canter, and lengthens its neck, the rider's hands should follow and go forward. If the horse strikes off on the correct leg, praise it. If it strikes off on the wrong leg, don't pull it up straight away, but let it take a few strides, then start again. After striking off two or three times, change the rein.

Page 35 top picture: The strike-off of a young horse from the trot. The rider pushes the inside pelvis bone forward. The outside hand is in contact, while the inside hand gives. The inside knee and heel are lowered, and go forward at the same moment the horse lifts its inside fore-leg. It is very important to do this at that precise moment. At the same time let the whip touch the shoulder slightly and say, 'Caaaanter!' Sit up straight and give a little with the reins. Lean back slightly to make it easier for the horse, and keep legs on in a minimal forward position. The outside hand is in constant contact, and the inside hand gives and takes.

Page 35 centre picture: **A** *The strike-off from the halt. Sit slightly behind the vertical. Hands in contact with the reins, lowered knee and heel.* **B** *Push the pelvis forward. The inside knee and heel are lowered, and go forward. The upper body is behind the vertical. Give with the reins until the horse strikes off, then keep contact.* **C** *The upper body is straight in the saddle. Seat and hands are in contact. The thigh is firmly on the horse to be able to push when necessary. Half-halt with the outside rein, holding with the inner. All is clearly shown in the sketches at the bottom of the page.*

Left **A** *The true footfalls in working canter* **B** *in collected canter* **C** *mainly in extended canter.*

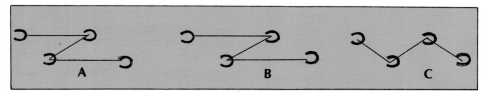

Transition from canter to trot
1 *When the outside hind-leg touches the ground the rider pushes his seat forward, his body back, lowers the knee and heel and has a strong contact with the reins. This brings the inner hind-leg under the horse, thereby lowering the hindquarters.*

2 *The horse touches the ground with the outside fore-leg and the inner hind-leg. The rider pushes his seat forward and lowers his knee. The hands continue their contact with the horse's mouth, but give a little. Be careful that the horse does not get too low in front, as transitions have that effect.*

3 *The horse 'lifts' itself again. The off-fore and near hind-leg start the trot steps. The rider uses his lower leg to urge the horse forward; the waist and hand follow the movement.*

Transitions

The rider has to pay special attention to the transitions. In competitions the judge looks particularly for smooth transitions.

The unschooled horse

When riding a young horse the transition from canter to trot is best made by sitting lightly and using a light contact with the horse's mouth. The slowing down is achieved with a giving and taking of the reins, combined with a light seat and the help of the voice saying 'Whoa'. When the horse has changed to trot the rider should rise, and at the same time rest his hands on the withers. It is easier this way to keep the horse on the bit. The first trot steps are often very

unbalanced, and throw the rider out of the saddle.

The schooled horse

When the horse is more balanced, and can carry its weight more easily, the rider can then ask for more in the transitions — from canter to trot, trot to walk, walk to halt, and also from canter direct to halt (*see picture above*).

Through sitting deep in the saddle and with the upper body slightly back, the rider can give stronger forward aids. At the same time the horse is asked to shorten its canter strides. The rider gives and takes with the reins, though the outside rein should be stronger, and at the same time the inside leg is back a

little. The inside rein stops the horse from leading with his inside shoulder. At the same time the inside leg helps to engage the horse's hindquarters. The transition therefore will be smoother. The outside rein and leg must stay in contact, otherwise the horse might change behind.

The basic rules for transitions are:

- Giving and taking of the reins with the inside rein always stronger.
- Forward-driving lower leg and seat with the inside leg slightly back.
- Don't forget your outside leg.

Rein-back

A horse has been properly worked if it goes willingly and correctly backward. The horse should step backward when the rider gives the correct aids, a light pressure with the lower leg behind the girth and a restraining hand. The rein-back, if properly executed, gives the impression of a forward movement. The well-schooled horse will go backward until it feels the rider's hand giving with the reins and a stronger leg.

It is easiest to teach a horse to rein back from the ground (*see picture on the right*). The instructor holds the bridle lightly, touches the fetlock of the nearest fore-leg and says, 'BAACK'. The horse will lift that leg as well as the diagonal hind-leg and step backward. The instructor should touch the near and off-foreleg in rhythm with the horse's steps and not make use of the bridle at all, so that the horse will go backward step by step.

If the horse is taught with a rider up, it is an advantage to have a helper who does the same as the instructor, but with only the rider using his voice. It is important to start with the leg and

shoulder which is farthest forward. The rider has his legs on the horse and a good contact with its mouth. When the horse lifts the forward foot with the help of the whip the rider's aid should be on the opposite side. The reins are in contact and there is light pressure with the legs. These aids should be used alternately to stop the horse from swinging to either one or the other side. Do not try to pull the horse back; keep your seat still, and do not lean back too far. You should sit straight or even perhaps a little forward without the seat coming out of the saddle. When this movement is properly carried out the horse lowers its hindquarters and the fore-legs are straight. The rein-back is a very good exercise for engaging the hindquarters, and helps the collection.

Above: Rein-back from the ground.

*Below: **A** and **B** the teaching of the rein-back. **A** right leg and right rein-change to **B** left leg and left rein, back to **A**, then **B** etc. Compare with the drawings on the right as seen from above.*
C The rein-back of the schooled horse. Firm hands and strong legs make the horse go backward. Compare with the picture as seen from above.

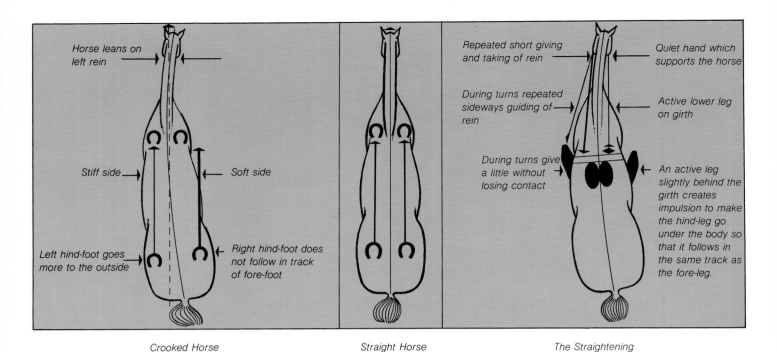

Horse leans on left rein

Stiff side

Soft side

Left hind-foot goes more to the outside

Right hind-foot does not follow in track of fore-foot

Crooked Horse

Straight Horse

Repeated short giving and taking of rein

Quiet hand which supports the horse

During turns repeated sideways guiding of rein

Active lower leg on girth

During turns give a little without losing contact

An active leg slightly behind the girth creates impulsion to make the hind-leg go under the body so that it follows in the same track as the fore-leg.

The Straightening

The straightening of the horse

It is impossible to carry out an exercise correctly on a crooked horse. One of the most important tasks of the rider is to straighten his horse.

With a few exceptions, it is usually the off hind-leg which the horse finds most difficult to bring under its body. It finds it uncomfortable to bend the off hind, and is inclined to put it down away from the body to the right. At the same time it pushes the near shoulder out and flexes to the left. The result is that the horse has a softer off-side and a stiffer near-side. It also leans more on the rein on the stiff side and pushes against the rider's left leg.

It is therefore very important to train the horse to put the off hind in a straight line to the off fore in all paces. If the rider manages this the horse will go evenly on both reins and be straight. When stiffness and resistance disappear the horse will give in its back and allow the rider to sit in the correct position.

Basic principles for straightening the horse

1. Straightening the horse must not interfere with its forward action. Do the work at a lively pace, but do not hurry.
2. The rider must definitely not try to straighten the horse by forcing it to bend to the stiff side. This will only increase its resistance, and result in greater stiffness and uneven paces.
3. Don't try to bend or straighten the horse when standing still, walking or at a slow pace. This will usually make it even stiffer.

Straightening the horse

Ride the horse forward, be active with both legs. Work in trot. Give and take with the reins on the stiff side so that the horse finds it difficult to lean on that side. At the same time keep the other rein steady and in contact so that the horse has support.

Make several turns towards the stiff side and take the rein away from the neck and towards your hip. It is even better to work the horse on a volte on its stiff side. The horse is made to go with the wrong bend with equal tension on both reins. It finds this uncomfortable, and slowly gives on the stiff side and accepts the outside rein. The body weight of the horse pushes it to the outside of the volte, so that it looks automatically for support from the outside rein.

The rider must watch out for this, and try to give what is asked for. Be careful not to have the rein away from the neck all the time. When the horse starts to accept the rein on the stiff side which it avoided up to now, this rein can be used to support the rider's leg on the soft side. The lower leg should be behind the girth to try to make the hind-leg come under the horse.

If one wants to be successful in dressage, it is essential for the horse to be straight. The basic principle demands that there is no tightening of muscles and tenseness. The whole horse must be relaxed.

Should the rider not pay attention to this important fact, and not get the horse straight, it will be tense in its body and stiff in its back and will not be able to flex its neck in the correct position.

Below: The straightening of the horse in the volte. **A** *There is an even contact with the reins, and both legs urge it forward into trot. The horse is allowed to have the wrong bend. The rein on the left, the stiff side, guides the horse into the volte, and the right leg, slightly back, drives it forward.* **B** *Gradually the horse will get tired of this uncomfortable position, though it may take several voltes, before this happens. It will start to alter and improve its flexion, and get the hind-legs more under the body in the direction of the fore-leg. At the same time it starts to soften on the stiff side and give in the neck. It relaxes in the poll and drops its head. The rider must watch out for this.* **C** *The hands remain the same with a firm contact and the legs keep driving the horse forward in the volte, though it is now more comfortable for the horse.*

When the horse goes happily, accepting the reins evenly on both sides, the rider goes straight with forward driving-aids.

Balance

For the horse to be able to execute difficult movements it must be able to move in fluid balance. This can only be achieved when it uses its back to get a forward impetus, through the engagement of the quarters and hind-legs under the body. This can only be achieved when it uses its back to get a forward impetus.

How will the rider manage this? He has to be in contact with the hind-quarters and push the hind-legs towards the centre of his own gravity so that they will (a) carry more weight and (b) be more active.

This is very difficult for the young horse, as its muscles will be resisting. It is therefore very important for the rider to build up the muscles in its hind-quarters. This is done step by step through dressage and getting the horse generally fit. The work consists of riding in undulating country, galloping, work over cavalletti, show-jumping, dressage and especially long-rein driving, which strengthens the hindquarters and shoulders. It is important that the work is varied, and it must be fun for the horse. The training must not be one-sided or boring.

Only after working the horse this way for several months will it develop strong muscles in its back which will give it cadence in its paces. The rider has the feeling that he is sitting on a softer horse. The paces will be relaxed and even, the steps longer and with more spring to them, and the horse will accept the hand of the rider more willingly.

A horse that is ridden with a strong seat and legs will use its back, lowering its hindquarters and bending the hind-legs at a more acute angle. The hind-legs go farther under the body, the back is rounded, the neck and head come up with the head in a vertical position. The centre of gravity is pushed back, and the hind-legs carry more weight. In this way the horse can achieve a fluid balance.

The rider must be certain that this balance is achieved by his leg-aids and not with the reins.

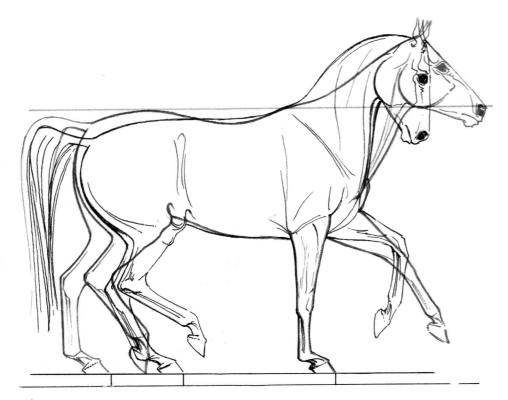

The difference between the unschooled, 'green' horse (green in the diagram) and the schooled horse (black in the diagram) is very great. Look how 'short' the schooled horse is. The back is higher, the croup is lower and the hind-legs are at an angle. The neck is raised and the horse gives in the poll. The steps are active, with cadence. The hind-legs are well under the body, and so can carry the weight more easily. The unschooled horse carries a good deal of weight on the forehand. By using its back the schooled horse pushes the centre of gravity back. This posture brings balance, and hence a greater chance for the horse to be able to carry out difficult movements.

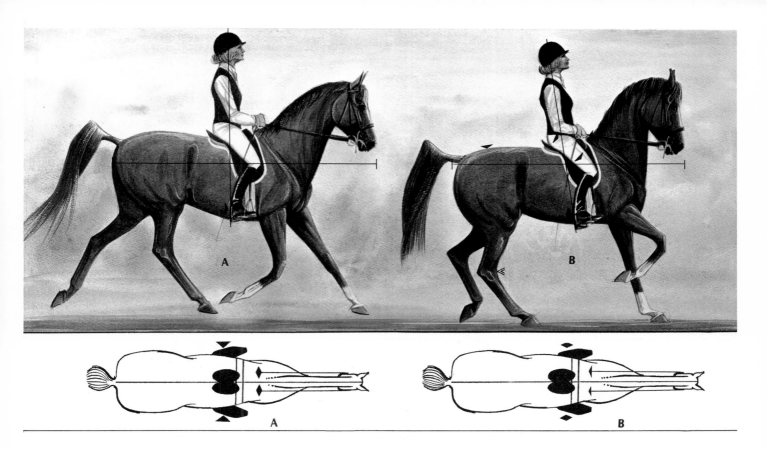

*Half-halt **A** The leg pushes the horse forward into the restraining hand. **B** The hands keep hold. The rider sits deeper in the saddle, and the knee is lowered. The leg is just in contact with the horse. The croup is lowered, the legs come farther under the body. Watch how the shift of the centre of gravity shortens the horse. Compare the picture with the sketches of the aids as seen from above.*

The half-halt

In the half-halt the horse shortens its steps and lowers its pace for a moment. The half-halt is used:
- To re-establish the horse's balance.
- To make the horse pay attention.
- To prepare it for the next movement.
- Repeated half-halts prepare the horse for the halt.

The half-halt is achieved by the rider sitting deeper in the saddle, a stronger leg and shortening of the reins. The body must not lean back too much, as too much weight will be put on the hind-legs and stop the horse's forward movement. The horse's hindquarters come more under its body, and it can balance better this way. The steps are more active, and smoother. If the horse leans on the bit, or resists, the rider should sit deeper in the saddle, use a stronger leg, and give and take with the reins.

When the rider gives the reins after the half-halt, it must not be exaggerated or hurried (definitely not a loose rein), as the horse will otherwise lose its collection and balance which was achieved through the half-halt.

Many riders would be a great deal more successful if they realized the importance of the half-halt, the way it helps to balance the horse and make it pay attention to the rider's wishes.

The halt. The rider keeps firm contact with the reins, sits deep in the saddle and increases the leg pressure. The horse lowers its hindquarters and bends its hocks. The rider continues his contact with the reins, sits deeper and keeps his legs well on. When the horse gives and stands the rider eases the reins but continues with the leg-pressure, so that it will halt correctly. Look for the change in the vertical line of the rider's body. Compare the picture with the sketch as seen from above.

The halt

To achieve a correct halt, horse and rider must be in complete accord, which is not easy and is demanding. The rider's reaction should be purely instinctive; he should feel what the horse is going to do, and give the appropriate aids.

The halt should be well prepared with one or two half-halts. The halt itself is a half-halt, which is continued with stronger restraining aids until the horse stops. As soon as the horse halts the rider should give with the reins so that the horse can stand squarely and evenly on all four legs. The balance should be slightly forward so that the hindquarters are not pushed under the body. The hind-legs must not move after the halt. If the horse does not halt correctly it is

better to ride on and halt again than to try to correct the halt. Praise the horse when it has been a good halt.

If one of the fore-legs is too much under the body the rider can nudge the horse on that same side with his lower leg, and give a little with the rein on that side.

When one of the hind-legs is left behind the rider can sense it, as that side is slightly lowered. As soon as the rider can feel this he should put his leg behind the girth on the same side. This touches the muscles on the horse's stomach, and makes them contract. The horse will lift his leg and move it forward. Take care, though, that neither fore or hind leg are moved too far for-

ward. Correction must always be made forward, not back.

It is necessary for the rider to keep a correct position, with the seat deep in the saddle and the heel lowered. The legs should be well on the horse, so that it will stay straight. Don't move your body forward, as your hands are likely to go forward too, and the leg back. The forward impetus then gets lost, and the hind-legs stay far behind. The horse will hollow its back.

In the halt the horse should keep the basic impetus and softness in its back and engagement of the hocks until the rider relaxes and sits completely still in the saddle.

Halt–Salute

When taking part in a competition, the rider enters on the centre line, halts and salutes the judge, who then returns the salute and the test begins. The finish of the test is also ridden on the centre line; the rider then halts and salutes, awaits the judge's acknowledgment and leaves the arena.

These are important movements in dressage competitions. It is difficult to get the horse straight, and to make it stay straight when saluting. These movements are correct if the horse stands quite still and its weight is evenly distributed on all four legs. The fore-legs should be straight, and the hind-legs roughly under the hip-bone.

The horse should be free in the shoulder and without tension in back and hindquarters, with the neck raised and giving in the poll. It should be on the bit. It can be difficult for the rider to feel whether the horse is square or not. If the points of the shoulder-blades are in line it is almost certain that its fore-legs are also in line. If one of the hind-legs is left behind that side of the horse is lowered, and one sits not quite straight in the saddle.

In the novice classes progressive transitions to the halt are permitted, such as trot, walk, halt or canter, trot, halt. As the tests increase in difficulty more accuracy is demanded. From Medium onward, the transitions have to be direct — for instance, from canter direct to halt.

If the horse finds it difficult to stand still in the halt the rider could lower his left hand without releasing the reins and press his small finger against the wither, or even scratch the horse with the reins. This usually helps to relax it, and make it listen to the rider.

When the rider salutes both reins are put into the left hand. The right hand is lowered and hangs straight down the rider's side. Lady riders lower their heads in salute. Gentlemen remove their hats and hold them at their side. Military riders give their salute in the usual way. When the judge has returned the salute the reins are quietly taken up and the test begins.

The pictures show a sideways view of one rider and the other as seen by the judge.

Dressage

Xenophon said, 'When a rider has managed to make his horse look as if it were free and showing off, then he is riding a horse that looks happy, proud and beautiful.'

This can never be forced.

The basic principles are looseness and softness. The horse must be quiet and straight, and willingly go forward when asked.

However beautiful the horse is, if it carries out its exercises without enthusiasm, in a dull and indifferent way, it will not be a pleasure to either rider or judge, and the judge will feel that it would look much better when moving freely in a field.

It is of course an advantage for the dressage horse to be well bred and with good conformation, but that is not a decisive factor, and must not be so. The important thing is the horse's movement. It should be supple and move freely, have balance and cadence, and be active from head to tail with spring in its paces.

The horse should carry out the rider's instructions in an elegant and smooth way. To do this it does not have to *be* beautiful, but when it has been made to carry itself in such a way that it *looks* beautiful, happy and proud the aim has been achieved, and that is DRESSAGE.

A well-adjusted pair

Ballet dancer–Dressage horse

When a horse goes in the highest collection, as it does in Piaffe and Passage, it must not be a question of force. Through its long period of all-round training, the horse should be so conditioned that it enjoys these movements, and its muscles are able to carry them out without strain. In other words, it moves as it would when free. It is so much in control of its body that it does not feel the weight of the rider on its back.

When a horse is free it can do flying changes, piaffe, passage and pirouettes without having been taught, but as soon as a rider is on its back the lightness of its movements vanishes. The weight on its back restricts it; it becomes clumsy and stumbles.

Slowly the horse has to be taught how to move with a rider on its back, and to build up its muscles. Gradually it will gain strength in its back and hindquarters, and the strain of carrying the rider will gradually diminish.

The foal follows its mother and groom in the 'kindergarten'. As a yearling and two-year-old, it starts 'school proper'. It then graduates to 'prep school' as a five-year-old, and then to grammar school. Now the horse is ready for 'university'.

Now the real dressage begins. The horse should now be able to achieve balance and equilibrium in the really difficult movements. The aids of the rider should be barely visible, and the horse must follow them without question.

Complete harmony between rider and horse is the aim. Rider and horse should complement each other and work in unison. This only *looks* easy!

Equipment

The dressage saddle must suit not only the rider but also the horse, and be very carefully fitted. The pommel and cantle should be the same height, with the lowest point of the saddle in between. The panel must be well stuffed. The saddle must not be allowed to press on the backbone of the horse. When the rider is sitting straight in the saddle the pressures should be evenly distributed over all parts of it that touch the horse.

The flap or skirt should be flat and relatively thin so that the rider's thigh can have a good contact with the horse. A numnah that is machine-washable is a good idea, as it will keep the saddle itself clean. There must be no creases in the numnah, and it must be well pulled up into the channel.

The saddle should be deep enough for the rider to sit comfortably and firmly. The flaps should be flat so that the rider's thighs can lie flat against them.

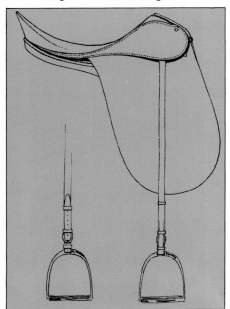

In order not to have the stirrup-leather buckle on the saddle one can have leathers as shown, though they are not generally used in England.

The buckle of the stirrup leather should be as shown: right at the top, or below.

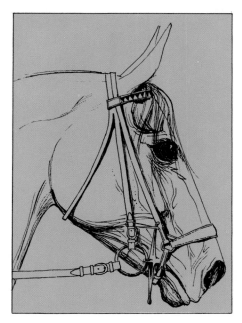

A small leather loop fixed to the headpiece keeps the cheek in position and gives leverage to the snaffle.

The snaffle-bit is important, but unfortunately the rider does not always appreciate this fact. It must fit the horse properly, and therefore be very carefully chosen. It must be neither too big nor too small. The snaffle is the correct size if one can see about 1cm between the bit and the corner of the horse's mouth. Generally a thick bit is the best, about 18 to 20cm thick.

The rider must take care that the bit is not too old, and that it has not got sharp edges, which could easily cut the horse's mouth. Have a good look at the whole bit, including the rings, to see that there are no sharp edges anywhere. It is possible to put bit-guards between the rings and the mouth, but these are not permitted in dressage tests. There are also bits with cheeks as in the picture above, which prevent the bit moving about in the mouth too much and help it to remain central in the mouth.

The **double bridle** consists of a curb bit and bridoon (i.e., snaffle). The action of this bit depends on the type. Thick bar and short cheeks — soft. Thin bar and long cheeks — sharp. The bridoon is fitted like an ordinary snaffle and lies in the mouth above the curb bit. The latter becomes effective when it assumes an angle of 45° in the mouth. Pressure is then brought to bear on the bars of the mouth and on the curb groove by means of the curb chain attached to the eyes of the bit. A certain downward pressure is also exerted on the poll through the cheekpiece attached to the bit.

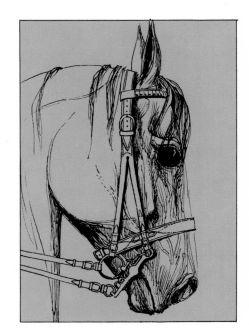

The bridle here has only one headpiece, which divides to hold the curb bit and bridoon, but it is not normally used in England.

Dressage at shows

The rider who takes his horse to a show for the first time must reckon with some difficulties. No one knows how the horse will react to all the new situations. It is easier to prepare a horse for shows when horse and rider have a little experience.

One problem (to which no one seems to be able to supply the answer) is how long to ride the horse in before the test. The horse should be obedient, so that the rider's aids are not obvious, but at the same time it must not be tired or it will lose its active paces and cadence. For the judge the willingness of the horse to go forward is as important as is obedience.

The rider has to pay attention to the following four points: the rider's seat and application of aids, the horse's paces, its willingness to go forward and its obedience and attention.

Attentiveness does not only mean obedience but the confidence the horse shows in the rider and the ease with which it executes the test.

The walk

The competitive rider often forgets the importance of the walk, which is as paramount as the 'advanced movements'.

The walk should be true, free, energetic and cover the ground. Each leg should move the same distance — e.g., both fore or hind-legs. The steps should be long and cover the ground. For footfalls see picture below. For description of walk as a pace and wrong footfalls see page 32.

A walk that is tense and not true usually stems from muscle tension, especially in the hindquarters. A frequent cause of this is the rider using a too strong outside rein. This makes the horse shorten its stride, especially behind. The hand does not give enough.

It depends entirely on the horse's stage of training how much collected walk the rider can ask for.

The collected walk can only be asked of a horse that has had several years of training and because of this can carry more weight on its hindquarters, and therefore be really active behind.

The rider regulates the degree of collection with alternate aids, giving and taking with hands and legs, so that the horse shows a nice active and balanced walk.

Walk on the long rein (A) Is a relaxed exercise in which the horse goes quietly with free shoulder movement on a completely loose rein. The feet overtrack. The neck is stretched but head not too low.

Medium walk (B) In this walk the rider has a light contact with the horse's mouth. The walk is active and the horse overtracks. The head can move a little in the rhythm of the walk.

Collected walk (C) More weight is put on the hind-legs. There is a more definite lifting of the legs and the steps are shorter. The hind-legs are put down behind the steps of the fore-legs. The hocks come under the horse and the quarters are lowered; at the same time head and neck are higher. The walk should be lively and regular.

Extended walk (D) Should cover as much ground as possible without being hurried or irregular. The steps should definitely overtrack. The head of the horse is given greater freedom.

Walk. The feet touch the ground in the following sequence: Near hind, near fore, off hind, off fore. One should clearly hear the four-time beat. The picture shows the off hind being lifted and put down while the off fore is lifted and then put down.

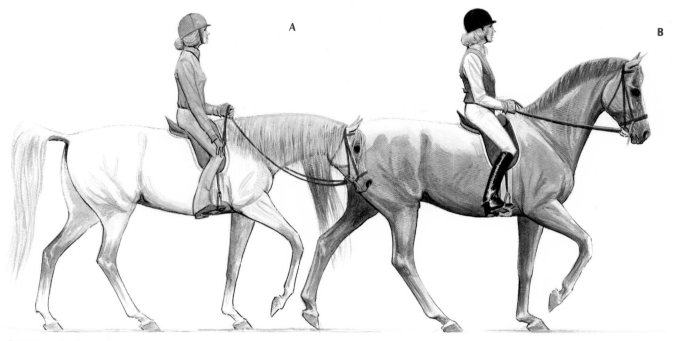

A *Walk on the long rein*

B *Medium walk*

C *Collected walk*

D *Extended walk*

The trot

The trot must be true and light as well as soft and rhythmic. The trot is a movement in two-time with the diagonal legs touching the ground at the same time (*for footfalls, see picture below; for faulty trot see page 33*). Only two steps should be heard. The trot is often in four-time when the horse is not balanced — for instance, if the hind-legs trail with too much knee action or wrong collection. The cause of this is too much hand and too little leg.

More trot than any other pace is used in dressage. The horse shows greater impulsion than in walk. Again it depends on the stage of the horse's education and training how much collected trot can be asked for. Working trot, shortened working trot and medium trot are asked for in tests up to and including Elementary. From Medium tests upward, collected trot is asked for, as well as extended trot.

Working trot (A) The working trot is an active and forward-going pace, a little more lively than the shortened working trot. The horse goes on a longer rein, with longer steps than in the shortened working trot. It is usually ridden rising. The hind-legs should be well engaged, and the fore-legs not stretched out too much.

Shortened working trot (B) is ridden mainly in the manège and sitting. The horse should be balanced and not tense, and the steps even. Position of horse and tempo must be in accordance with the horse's education. The horse should accept the bit willingly and go forward into it. If the bit is too severe or ill-fitting, and the rider's hands too harsh, the horse will try to evade the bit and go behind it, and the nose will come behind the vertical. The steps will be tense and the hind-legs not engaged, and the horse will go more with a stiff and hollow back. The transition from working to shortened working trot should be clearly defined without jolting the horse, which is not ready for collected work until it can carry out the less advanced movements in a smooth and correct way, helped by aids that are hardly discernible.

Before the aids for collection can be effective, the horse must be obedient without being tense, must understand the aids and accept the bit without resistance on both reins. Should the rider ask for too much collection when the horse is not ready for it, it will resist by going behind the bit or not engaging the hindquarters and going wide behind.

Collected trot (C) The difference in the shortened working trot and the collected trot is a slower tempo and slight suspension, which is achieved by the horse using itself more, and the hind-legs coming farther under the body. The hindquarters are lowered, the movements in the shoulder become more free, and the head and neck are raised. The action of the legs is not only forward but upward in suspension. This makes the steps more active and springy. Collected trot is used mainly in lateral work.

To get the transition from shortened working trot to collected trot, the rider sits heavier in the saddle with a straight back and pushes his pelvis slightly forward with his body still straight. The lower leg is behind the girth to ask the horse to go forward, as well as asking for collection. Giving and taking of the outside rein slows the horse down and lets it transfer the centre of gravity to the hindquarters. The horse must have a spring in its steps. It should accept the bit but not go behind it, as the freedom of the steps would be reduced. The rider must not lean back.

Extended trot (D) The extended trot is notable for its lengthening of steps, cadence of steps, free shoulder movement and hindquarters truly engaged. The tracks of the diagonal footfalls should be parallel, and there should be a definite suspension noticeable in each step taken (*See pages 52-3.*)

The footfalls in trot: **1** *Diagonal legs — right hind — left fore.* **2** *Suspension.* **3** *Diagonal legs: left hind — right fore are put down.* **4** *Suspension.* **5** *Right hind — left fore are put down again.*

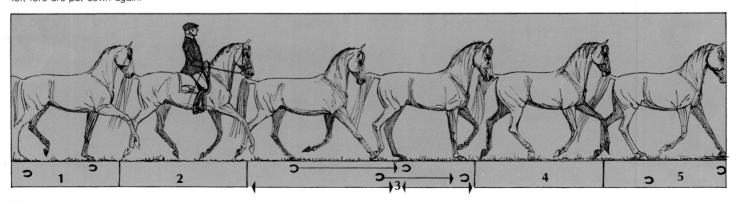

A *Working trot*

B *Shortened working trot*

C *Collected trot*

D *Extended trot*

Extended trot

The characteristics of the extended trot are:
- Substantially longer strides
- Energetic strides
- Free shoulder
- Parallel track of the diagonal steps (**A**)
- A definite suspension

The rider can only ask for a good extended trot when the horse's back muscles have been built up, and it can really engage its hind-legs. It must be trained to the point where it can shift the centre of gravity to the hindquarters, so that the shoulders are free and make it possible for the fore-legs really to stretch out, so that there is a true lengthening of the steps. The longer the

horse is in suspension, the better can it stretch its fore-legs and bend the hocks while it is in the air, before the hoofs touch the ground again.

When the horse is able to use its back and hind-legs without tension and with a spring in its steps, the rider will then be able to follow the horse's movements more easily without interfering with its back (**C**). The horse should be able to stretch its neck a little without losing contact with the rider's hand. This contact must be kept, but the neck can stretch a little and the nose come slightly in front of the vertical (*see picture above*). If the horse is behind the bit the steps will be running. It must not lean on the bit, otherwise the centre of gravity is transferred to the forehand. The horse often stumbles if the weight is on the forehand, as it cannot lift its fore-leg before the hind-leg touches the ground. Gentle giving and taking of the rein, alternating with a firm contact, will prevent the horse from leaning on the bit.

*In the extended trot the angle of the diagonal legs should be parallel (**A**).*

These four pictures show the steps in the trot with transition to extended trot. The last picture shows the moment of suspension.

If the horse should break into a canter because the rider is giving too strong aids, or from uneven ground, or because it is not on the bit, it should be brought back into trot immediately with the inside leg and rein. Use strong leg and firm rein to make the horse go forward again, and give in the suspension to get it back into extended trot.

The rider's seat

In the extended trot the rider's seat should be soft, and follow the movements. The legs are straight on the girth with a low heel (**B**) and strong forward aids. The rider should sit in the middle of the saddle with back and diaphragm softly following the movements (**C**). The seat in this position does not act as a forward driving-aid. It acts as such when the rider uses a strong back. Hands are low, and follow the movements without losing contact.

The teaching of the extended trot

The best way to start teaching the horse extended trot is when returning home after a hack. The horse will want to go forward to get home and will be in a relaxed state of mind.

Start with rising trot, with legs relatively forward on the girth, giving the aids in rhythm of the trot and a strong seat and back. Keep the horse's head fairly high, with short half-halts if it comes too low. The hands should have a good contact, with one hand perhaps

resting on the wither.

Trot as slowly as possible in a good rhythm, but with a little suspension, and try by strong forward aids to get the horse to lengthen its strides and come from behind. When the weight is slowly transferred to the hindquarters, and the horse is really carrying the rider, it will not stumble any more.

When the horse has gradually learned to lengthen its strides and carry the rider without tension, then is the time for the rider to sit in the trot.

The horse has to learn to make the transitions to the extended trot quickly. In a test it should start straightening when it comes off the long side on to the diagonal. To slow the horse down, the rider puts his leg back, sits upright and at the same time has a firm but not rigid contact with the reins.

*The two most important points of the rider's seat in the extended trot are (**B**) a long leg and (**C**) a soft and supple back and diaphragm.*

The canter

The canter when true is a light, energetic, animated movement with a moment of suspension. This depends on the speed and the collection of the horse (*see picture on bottom of page 55 and canter diagram on page 34*).

The horse should be straight when striking off in the canter. If it strikes off on two tracks the cause is usually a too strong and too far back outside leg. The rider must get the horse straight, and this is done through an active outside leg and a sideways pushing inside leg.

If the horse should lean too heavily on the bit the rider's hands must soften and give. He should give repeated half-halts, preferably with the outside rein to help the horse carry itself.

Canter from the trot

The rider shortens the trot strides, sits on his inside seat-bone, puts the outside leg back and flexes the horse slightly to the inside. The horse canters on when the outside hind-leg and the inside fore-leg touch the ground, takes a small stride and puts the outside hind-leg down again and continues in canter.

Canter to the trot

When in the second canter stride the inside hind-leg and the outside fore-leg touch down simultaneously the horse starts trotting, and with a jerk the opposite diagonal legs move forward.

Transition from canter to walk

The rider shortens the canter strides mainly with the inside rein, the inside seat-bone and the leg slightly back. In the moment of suspension he uses a stronger back and hands. When the horse puts down its outside hind-leg the rider stops giving canter aids. The horse will come lower, the outside hind-leg is lifted and the outside fore-leg starts the walk. The rider eases the reins so that the horse can lengthen its neck and move its head (*see page 36*).

Transition from walk to canter

The horse can make the transition from walk to canter when the sequence of the footfalls in the walk correspond with the ones in the canter. The moment before the horse puts down the inside fore-leg, it supports itself with the inside hind-leg and the outside fore-leg. It supports itself the same way in the canter. In the transitions to canter it pushes with the hind-leg at the same time as it steps with the inside fore-leg, makes a short leap, lands with the outside hind-leg and then continues in canter.

The collection in canter is gradually developed as the horse's education progresses, and when it achieves an even rhythm in all paces.

Disunited canter is wrong. In this canter the horse is on the right rein in front and on the left rein behind, or vice versa. The disunited canter is very uncomfortable for the rider, as the back of the horse is twisting all the time. Young horses often go disunited as they have not yet learned to go properly balanced. This is especially so when doing a flying change; it only changes with the hind-legs or in counter-canter if the rider has not asked for enough collection and positioned the horse properly. Stop cantering as quickly as possible and start again.

Below: The horse is cantering in four-time — outside hind, outside fore, inside hind, inside fore. The horse hollows its back, does not bend its hocks and resists in neck and sets its jaw. It is quite unbalanced, with its head high and a U neck. To begin with the rider has to try to lower the horse's head by giving and taking with the reins. Stronger leg aids should be employed to make the horse use its hind-legs, and these also help to bring its head down. The rider should then give repeated half-halts to try to make the horse carry itself better, and give in the neck.

Working canter (A) This pace is mostly ridden in the manège. Head and neck position correspond with the degree of training. The rider sitting straight in the saddle should follow the horse's movements, be supple, have the horse on the bit and balanced. Canter quietly and in true canter.

Collected canter (B) This canter can only be asked of a well-schooled horse. The difference between the working canter and the collected canter is a higher head and neck position, with the hocks coming more under the horse, increased cadence and liveliness of steps, though at a slower pace.

Extended canter (C) This is used in the manège to get the horse used to going forward. The speed and horse's outline depend on the stage of its education. The horse should be balanced, with a long springy stride. The rider sits in the saddle following the horse's movements.

Medium canter A pace not as fast as the extended canter but also balanced, with the horse bringing its hocks well under the body and long strides. This pace is frequently asked for in tests from Medium upward. A little more roundness should be shown than in the extended canter.

Counter-canter

This demands that the horse is well balanced, supple and obedient to the aids. The rider must show increased adaptability and careful co-ordination of the aids, especially when not riding a straight line, when most of the

*A Collected canter on left rein **B** Collected canter on right rein **C** Extended canter on right rein.*

Footfalls in canter on left rein

difficulties of the counter-canter occur.

The inside rein should be stronger, giving and taking with the outside rein which guides the horse when turning, but bent in the opposite direction to which the horse is going. The horse is inclined to go faster and transfer the centre of gravity forward. The rider must not be too strong with his hands or give too forceful aids, such as having too strong an inside rein or using the outside leg too much. Don't try to turn the horse by pressing the inside rein against its neck. Use the leading outside rein in the turn.

There are several ways in which the horse can be made to go in counter-canter (*see picture right*), such as changing the rein without changing leg back to the long side or through the circle. It is best, though, to teach the horse counter-canter through the following method:

The horse will be made to come off the long side after being ridden through the corner in collected trot. While in the loop it is asked to canter right **A** (*diagram right*). When it returns to the long side it will be in counter-canter. The loops should be gradually reduced until the horse strikes off in counter-canter on a straight line.

One can also arrive at counter-canter by going across the diagonal but making it shorter than usual and carrying on in a counter-canter circle. This exercise should be done quietly, without hurry and on the bit.

When the horse goes happily through corners and in circles in counter-canter the strike off can be practised at shorter and shorter intervals. This is a preparation for the flying changes.

Flying changes

This asks for a straight and balanced horse. It must be obedient and attentive to the rider's aids, be light in the mouth and active in its paces. The rider's seat must be firm, as well as accompanying the horse's movements, so that the aids can be definite.

The flying change takes place in the moment of suspension. When the horse canters on the right rein the horse reacts in the following way to the rider's aids: after the moment of suspension the

*Above: Counter-canter. Right leg leading on the left rein; the pair to be found at point **X** in the picture below.*
*Below: Suggestions for teaching flying changes, difficulties successfully increased. **A** On the right rein changing through the circle. **B** Changing through the counter-canter. **C** Changing through the diagonal.*

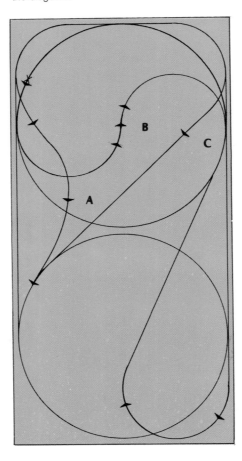

horse puts down the right hind-leg instead of the left and continues in the left canter, having also changed in front. The horse should stay straight and not swing to either side. The change must happen in one stride, the same rhythm and length of a normal canter stride.

The rider's aids must be given in good time, so that the horse is able to move the inner legs forward during the suspension. The aid for the new inner leg must be given at the precise moment, exactly when the horse puts down the inner fore-leg. The outer hind-leg has started its moment of suspension and the inner hind-leg just left the ground.

The sequences on top of page 57 show how the flying change works; here from right to left leg. The sketches with the horse seen from above show the rider's aids. The horse is in collected canter on the right rein. The rider sits firmly in the saddle with his weight mainly on the right (inside) seat-bone. The horse is straight, but with a slight bend to the right. When the horse puts the outside hind-leg down, after the moment of suspension, the rider moves his outside, right, leg back (**A**). When the horse puts down its inside fore-leg (**B**) the rider gives the aid with his outside leg against the side of the horse. The rider stays with more weight on his inside seat-bone, and at the same time puts some pressure on the inside rein to let the horse put down its new outside (right) hind-leg. This is quickly followed by an easing of this rein, and at the same time a stronger contact with the new inside rein (**C**).

The horse has learned earlier on to strike off in the canter with a strong inside rein. If it has a good contact with the rein it is easier for it to change during the suspension phase. The rider has to have a supple and flexible waist not to be lifted out of the saddle when during the change the horse lifts the side which becomes the inside so that it is able to move the leg forward. The rider's left leg, which becomes the inner leg, lies still and close to the horse's side, well down in the stirrup.

Immediately after the flying change, the rider changes position to the inner (left) seat-bone with the leg in position

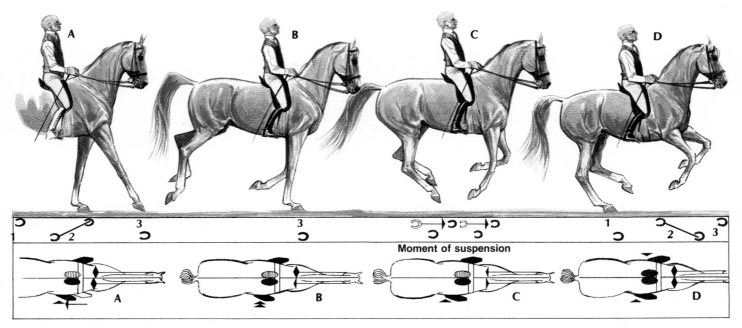

Flying change. Footfalls and aids.

for the left canter (**D**).

There are various methods of teaching the horse flying changes, and different methods have to be used for different horses. One of the methods is, as mentioned before, to prepare the horse by riding counter-canter. It is usually easiest for the horse to learn flying changes by riding a half-circle in counter-canter, then change (*see picture on page 56*). The place where the change is asked for should be varied all the time so that the horse does not start to anticipate. When the horse has done a good flying change it should be ridden forward in the canter so that it understands that it has done it well and is being rewarded.

The next step is to ask for the flying change through the circle. The circle should be about 20m diameter so that the horse is straight when changing, and should be asked for the change when the two half-circles meet (*see diagram on page 56*). The horse, for example, is on the left rein in canter, the rider trots a few steps when the half-circles meet, then asks for canter right.

The trot-steps are gradually reduced until the horse understands that the rider is asking for a flying change.

The horse must not be 'thrown around' by excessive rein and leg aids. The change to the new inside rein must be soft, and the horse must remain on the new outside rein. The rider must not change his position too quickly in the change or he makes it difficult for the horse to move the new inside leg forward.

The other method is to change through the diagonal and ask for the change when getting to the other long side. It should be given the new inside bend about two steps before asking for the change. If the horse is in canter right the right rein, which will be the outside rein, is pressed against its neck to help it change in front. The right leg, which has been placed behind the girth before the change, gives a strong aid when the right fore-leg touches the ground, and the rider then moves his seat gently to the left.

Frequent rider errors:
- Leaning forward.
- Moves too quickly and strongly to the inside seat-bone.
- Too strong leg-aids.
- Moving the leg which becomes the outside leg back too late.

1   2   3   4   5   6

Flying changes through leg-yielding and half-passes

In the Zig-Zag the horse should be ridden so that the angles formed by the directional changes are open and not by any means acute. The rider uses the same aids as in half-passes (*see page 68*), which are much the same as those for the canter. It is best to start in collected trot. When the horse has been going forward and sideways, and is within 4m of the track, the rider then changes the flexion to the opposite direction, stays on the same seat-bone and uses his leg on the same side to move the horse sideways and forward in the new direction and with a sideways rein. In the transition the horse is ridden in leg-yielding with flexion. It finds it easier to put its new outside hind-leg down when this movement is done in canter.

Make the angles increasingly open and decrease the canter strides on each side of the centre line until the horse changes on the straight line.

The exercise of riding Zig-Zags gradually forms one of the movements in advanced dressage tests (*see drawing on right*). Look at the position of the horse. To get the right number of strides on each side, the horse has to have more bend from head to tail than it would in a correct half-pass. The rider sits a little more strongly, with the inside seat-bone and with hip and body forward in the direction of the movement until the horse has changed legs. He then sits easily on the new outside seat-bone and keeps the horse in position with outside rein and leg. In the change

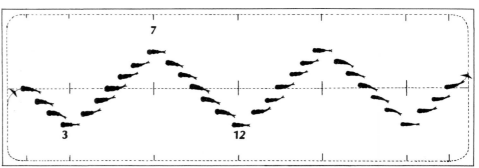

Zig-Zag Half-passes = Three strides right in canter, change, six strides left canter, change, six strides right canter, change, six strides left canter, change, six strides right canter, change, three strides left.

Look for the canter change at 3, 7 and 12. You can see how the horse is positioned and how it is straight in the changes.

Below: Footfalls and aids in the 'one-time' changes. Watch how the rider 'floats' above the saddle.

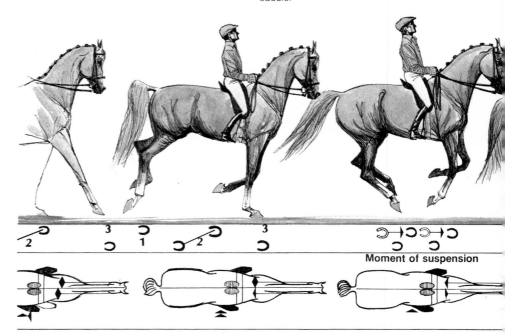

Moment of suspension

| 8 | 9 | 10 | 11 | 12 | 13 |

the horse should be straight. The body of the rider shifts the centre of gravity to the new direction, and the inside rein leads the horse's forehand.

Flying changes every stride

When the horse has learned four-time tempi (four strides left rein, four strides right rein) and three-time tempi (three strides left, three strides right) it can then be taught the two-time changes. Here the horse does two strides on the left leg, change, then two strides on the right leg. This is difficult for the horse, and in a way artificial, and tires it to begin with. In spite of this, 'one-time changes' have to be learned as well. The picture series below shows how and when the aids should be given. Canter changes each stride are one of the most difficult dressage movements. It is not possible to say exactly how they should be ridden, as individual ability of horse and rider and temperament play a large part. The aids for the changes at each stride are like a chain-reaction. The rider should sit very lightly, almost float above the saddle, and give the aids only with rein and leg. The horse has to lift its body on the inner side so that the inner legs can move forward. The inner and the outer side change with each stride. If the rider sits on his seat-bone he invariably gets pushed up. Transfer weight of body more on to thighs and knee and stirrup. Seat hardly in the saddle.

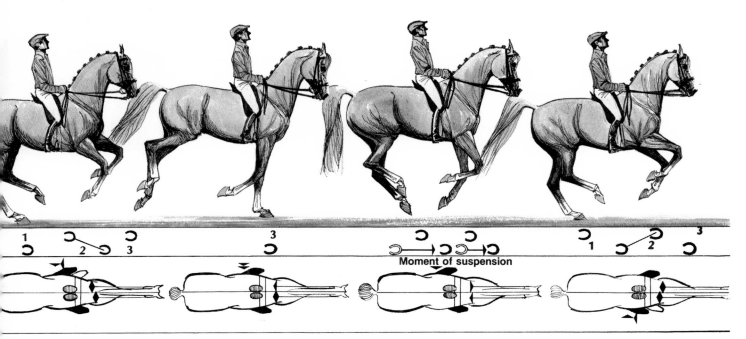

Moment of suspension

Changes of direction

These are usually carried out in the shape of a circle and are used to make the horse accept and follow the rider's aids given with changing his weight, and practise the co-ordination of these with the other aids, as well as improving the horse's collection. The horse has come a long way if it can execute a full turn on the haunches in collection and with active steps.

Small half-circle on the haunches

This follows a half-halt. The rider has a strong contact with the reins (a little stronger with the outside one) to act on the outside hind-leg. The rider uses an active leg to retain the horse's forward urge, definite footsteps and collection. He changes weight by lowering the inside heel and looks in the direction he is

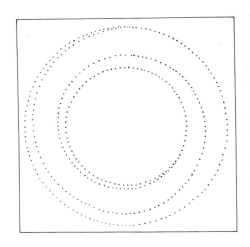

Decreasing and increasing the circle.

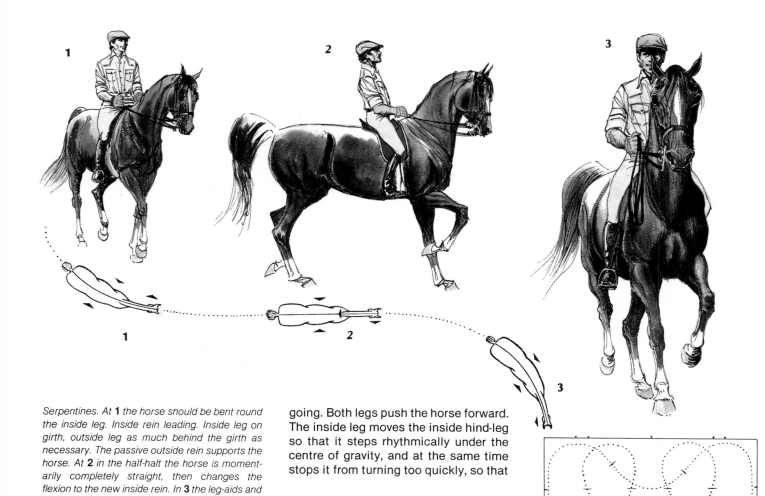

*Serpentines. At **1** the horse should be bent round the inside leg. Inside rein leading. Inside leg on girth, outside leg as much behind the girth as necessary. The passive outside rein supports the horse. At **2** in the half-halt the horse is momentarily completely straight, then changes the flexion to the new inside rein. In **3** the leg-aids and weight are changed. The new outside rein supports the horse. The serpentines will show whether the horse is straight, and how far the rider has succeeded in making it really straight.*

going. Both legs push the horse forward. The inside leg moves the inside hind-leg so that it steps rhythmically under the centre of gravity, and at the same time stops it from turning too quickly, so that

Right: Examples of serpentines. Notice the S shape of the loops. The little notches indicate the half-halts and change of flexion.

it turns step by step. The outside leg stops the outside hind-leg from falling away. The inside rein guides the horse in the direction asked for and the outside rein determines the size of the circle and stops the horse's quarters from falling out. After the circle the rider gives with the reins, straightens the horse and rides forward.

Riding through corners is equivalent to a quarter-circle and should be ridden accurately with the same aids as described previously (*also on page 28*). The volte is a small circle (6m) and again the same aids are used as before. When riding decreasing circles, as shown in the sketch at the top of page 60, the inside rein leads into the circle and at the same time the outside rein supports the outside leg. The horse's outline should follow the circle from head to tail. The outside rein controls. When enlarging the circle the outside rein leads the horse on to the bigger circle.

Turn on the haunches

These should be done in walk. The horse should turn round the inside hind-leg, which may describe a very small circle so that the forward movement is not lost. The transition from trot and canter to walk before and after the turns should be smooth, and flow from one into the other. When doing the turn on the haunches from the collected trot, the aids for the halt should be given so that the horse walks and the rider starts the turn at the same moment. The same method is used when the turn on the haunches is asked for from the collected canter.

When striking off in the canter after the turn on the haunches the rider must change his weight and change the horse's flexion. It is easier after the turn to start in counter-canter, as the rider does not have to change aids or position.

A turn on the haunches in trot means that the horse is virtually doing piaffe, and when it does it in canter it is a half or full pirouette and demands very careful preparation and training. The horse has to be really straight and collected, and has to be completely obedient to the rider's aids.

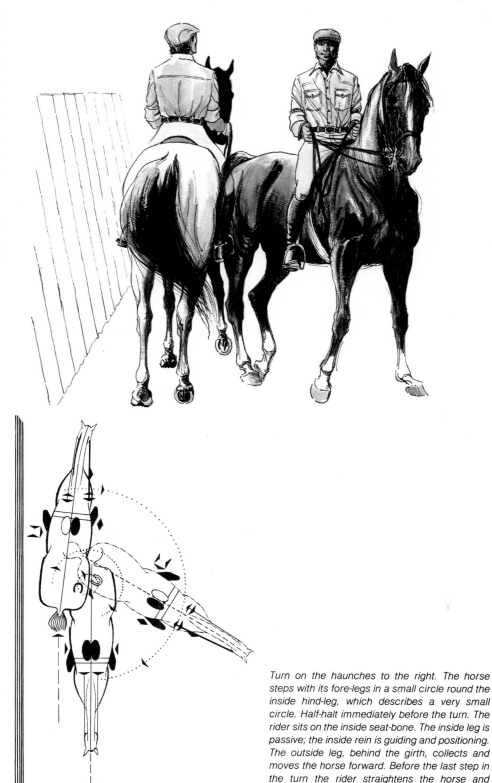

Turn on the haunches to the right. The horse steps with its fore-legs in a small circle round the inside hind-leg, which describes a very small circle. Half-halt immediately before the turn. The rider sits on the inside seat-bone. The inside leg is passive; the inside rein is guiding and positioning. The outside leg, behind the girth, collects and moves the horse forward. Before the last step in the turn the rider straightens the horse and pushes it forward with seat (same pressure on both seat-bones) and legs (both legs on girth).

Pirouette

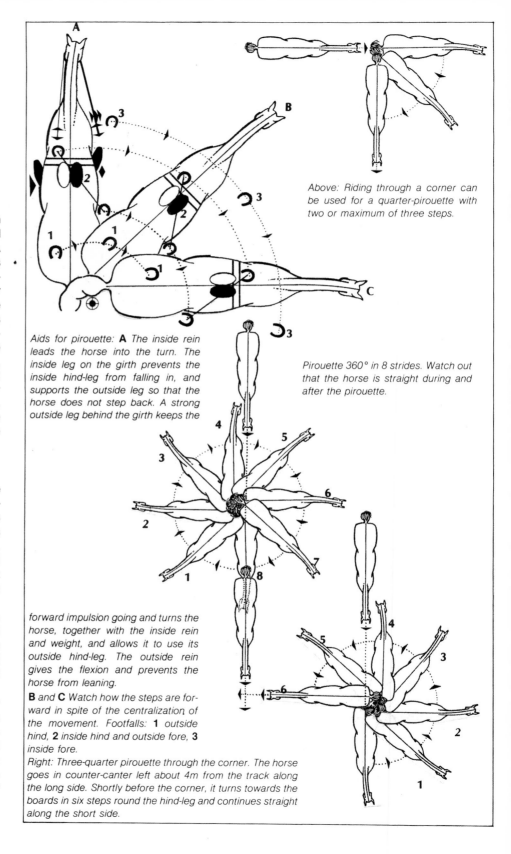

This is a full circle on the hind-legs in the canter. It is a turn of 360° and should be executed in six to eight strides. A three-quarter pirouette is 270° and is done in four to six strides, and a half-pirouette is 180° and three to four strides. The horse should turn round the inside hind-leg, which steps more or less on the spot, with both fore-legs and outside hind-leg. The horse should keep the canter rhythm and remain in collection, the flexion in direction of the turn and hocks well bent. The three-time canter stride must be kept going all the time. The rider must see to it that the horse can stay in full balance throughout the exercise.

The teaching of the pirouette

The best way to teach the half-pirouette and the full pirouette is through the half-pass or a half-volte. The half-volte is gradually made smaller until the horse's inner hind-leg stays on the same spot. This can only be done in a very collected canter. The horse must be able to do a half-pirouette correctly, before one can start to teach it the full pirouette.

Every detail of the earlier education has to be understood by the horse, and it must be able to do the exercises correctly. It must be really straight and accept the aids without resentment, and not tense up.

The pirouette can also be taught by riding a small volte (circle) with quarters in. The volte is slowly decreased. The horse must always be going forward and the rider be able to ride straight on at any given moment. To teach the horse the pirouette on a straight line, the rider rides in counter-canter along the long side of the manège (*see diagram, bottom*

Above: Riding through a corner can be used for a quarter-pirouette with two or maximum of three steps.

Aids for pirouette: **A** *The inside rein leads the horse into the turn. The inside leg on the girth prevents the inside hind-leg from falling in, and supports the outside leg so that the horse does not step back. A strong outside leg behind the girth keeps the*

Pirouette 360° in 8 strides. Watch out that the horse is straight during and after the pirouette.

forward impulsion going and turns the horse, together with the inside rein and weight, and allows it to use its outside hind-leg. The outside rein gives the flexion and prevents the horse from leaning.

B *and* **C** *Watch how the steps are forward in spite of the centralization of the movement. Footfalls:* **1** *outside hind,* **2** *inside hind and outside fore,* **3** *inside fore.*

Right: Three-quarter pirouette through the corner. The horse goes in counter-canter left about 4m from the track along the long side. Shortly before the corner, it turns towards the boards in six steps round the hind-leg and continues straight along the short side.

Pirouette to the left. The horse is at the end of the suspension phase. The first foot down is the out-side (right) hind-leg, then the inside (left) hind-leg, the outside (right) fore-leg and last the inside (left) foreleg. The second stride goes well forward and left and the third farther left and forward. The in-side hind-leg must not move too much to the side. The centre of the pirouette should be in or just behind the track of the inside hind-leg. The more the hocks are engaged the lighter it will be in the hand. The rider must be sympathetic with the reins and not put too much weight on the hind-quarters by leaning back.

right). Shortly before the short side the horse is made to canter almost on the spot and then ridden into the corner in a half-pirouette, and later on into a three-quarter pirouette. To begin with it is allowed to describe a small circle with its hind-legs, but subsequently the de-mand for more collection and balance is increased. The most difficult part is to judge the right pace. If it is too quick the horse cannot get its hind-legs suf-ficiently under the body. If it is too slow it will lose its canter stride. Slowly the horse will learn to do the pirouette on the centre line.

Leg-yielding and lateral work

Leg-yielding serves as a preparation for the half-passes. Leg-yielding is ridden in working trot or in canter, half-passes in collected trot or canter.

Leg-yielding is used to supple the horse, half-passes to collect it. There has to be increased balance when the horse is ridden on two tracks. The response of the horse to the rider's aids must be heightened. The half-pass is used as an exercise to improve the bend in the horse's body and to make the hind-quarters more supple and stronger, as well as freeing the shoulder and ensuring the acceptance of the reins and leg-aids. To establish the balance, this work is done with impulsion and even rhythm.

Half-passes should only be ridden for a few steps at the beginning, alternating with going forward in a straight line. The whole school or a large circle should be used to retain the rhythm of the steps. This will help the horse to move freely and smoothly in the half-passes.

Leg-yielding

In this movement the horse's head and neck are flexed opposite to the way it is going. The body is straight, and it is on two tracks away from the inside leg (the leg opposite to the horse's flexion). The movement starts with a half-halt and should be carried out with some collection. The horse is positioned contrary to the direction it will be going, and before it is asked to go sideways. It is a bad mistake if the hindquarters are leading. The horse should be moved in the direction the rider wants it to go, and he applies both legs on the girth to keep the impulsion going. The inside leg supports the rein on the same side and moves the horse sideways. The inside lower leg must never be passive or cling to the horse but be active all the time and move in rhythm with the reins on the same side. If the rider wants to move the hindquarters he should put his lower leg behind the girth; slightly forward when he wants to move the forehand. The outside lower leg makes the horse go forward; at the same time he uses the outside rein to prevent the horse from falling on its shoulder. The outside rein is the guiding rein. It is important that the horse reacts to the leg-aids and does not lean on the hand.

Leg-yielding is not easy. The aids have to change the whole time between asking for forward movement, for sideways movements, guiding, supporting and holding. The horse will tense up if too much angle is asked for, or if the rider gives the wrong diagonal aids. The movement is correct if the horse is relaxed. It is most important to be active and have impulsion in this exercise.

The rider has to learn the feel of the horse giving and straight away give himself likewise, especially the inside rein.

When finishing the leg-yielding, the horse is straightened, the hind-legs on the same track as the fore-legs, and it is ridden forward at a faster pace. The rider should feel the increased pace and the horse taking more hold of the bit.

This should first be practised in the walk, but later on it is ridden mainly in

A *Leg-yielding, the horse bent away from the way it is going.* **B** *Half-pass. The horse is bent the way it is going, and curved round the inside leg.* **C** *Shoulder-in. The horse's body and neck are bent away from the direction it is going, and it is on three tracks.* **Da** *Renvers (left);* **Db** *Travers (right).*

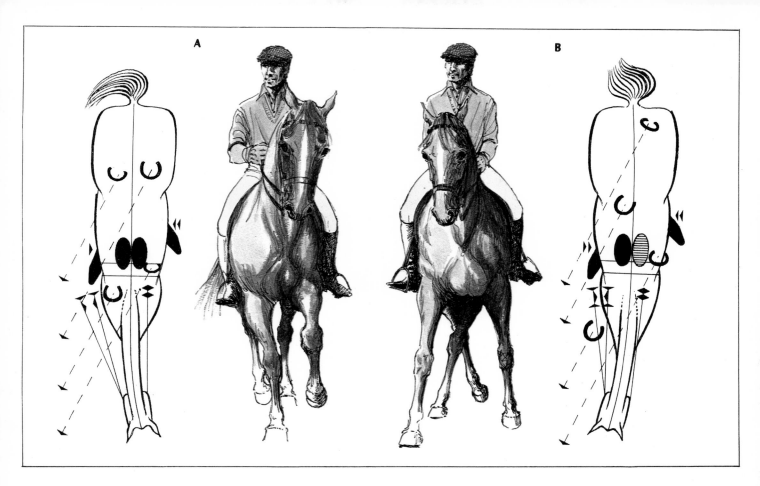

A   B

trot, as it is easier to keep the horse going forward. The steps are even, and the diagonal legs move at the same time.

Half-pass

In the half-pass the horse's flexion is in the direction it is going.

It should also be slightly bent round the rider's inside leg. The half-pass, like leg-yielding, is ridden mostly in trot.

It is easiest for the horse to learn the half-pass when ridden out of a half-volte as it is already bent in the right direction. The aids for the half-volte are almost the same as those for the half-pass. The added aid is the sideways-forward driving outside lower leg. To make the horse more attentive to the sideways-forward aids, the rider can start with a very small volte, almost a turn on the haunches. The horse, which is then parallel with the long side, is ridden forward into the half-pass. A half-

pass can also be started after riding well into the corner where the horse has already the right bend.

The rider sits more on the inner seat-bone, where the weight is shifted in the direction of the movement. Both lower legs are on the horse, and keep the forward impulsion going. The aids on the inside help to bend the horse's neck and body, the leg is on the girth, the reins guiding and supporting, the hand opposite the rider's inside hip. The outside lower leg is behind the girth, and drives the horse sideways. The rein stops the horse from bending its neck more than its body: the rider should look in the direction he is going. The horse should go forward and sideways with active strides.

When the half-pass is finished the rider stops giving the sideways aids with the outside leg. He eases the leading rein and rides the horse forward on a straight line.

The horse is positioned for lateral work and bent round the inside leg. **A** *Leg-yielding.* **B** *Half-pass. The horse is positioned more or less the same in both exercises, but watch for the head and neck position.* **A** *In leg-yielding the horse's head and neck are bent in the opposite direction to which it is going, with a nearly straight body. The horse lifts the left fore-leg up straight and right hind-leg. The rider drives the horse forward with his weight in the middle of the saddle. The right lower leg is slightly back, and acts as forward driving aid and stops the horse from leading with the shoulder. The left leg, slightly back, makes the horse go sideways and keeps the impulsion going. Outside (right) rein guides the horse and keeps it going in the right direction. The inside rein keeps the horse's bend.* **B** *In the half-pass the horse bends in the direction it is going and a little rounded. The rider sits more on the inside seat-bone. The horse lifts the right hind-leg up straight and the left fore-leg. The aids of legs and hands are the same as in leg-yielding.*

Exercises in lateral work

These are used to make the horse supple, not only in his body but in the joints of the hind-legs. When suppleness has been achieved it makes it much easier for the horse to transfer the centre of gravity behind the saddle, and in this way get greater collection. The shoulders are freer, and the horse is higher in front. Submission to hand and leg aids is increased.

Shoulder-in

In this movement the horse should be slightly bent from head to tail against the direction it is going. The inside leg should step in front of the outside one. The horse is collected with diagonal aids, mainly the inside lower leg and outside rein. The outside lower leg is always stronger to push the outside hind-leg under the horse. This necessitates that the inside crossing

hind-leg be also well underneath.

The inside lower leg activates the sideways movement, the outside one restrains. The reins position and bend the horse, the outside rein directs the way the horse is going (*see also picture on opposite page*). The rider must not collapse in the waist, and the inside rein must not be too strong and restraining.

It is advantageous to start the shoulder-in out of a corner as the horse is bent already in the right direction. The rider's aids are mainly the same, and the horse has the long wall for support. After riding accurately through the corner the rider gives a half-halt, then leads the fore-legs off the track, gives another half-halt and then rides the horse sideways and forward in the shoulder-in movement and gets more collection through stronger leg-aids and firm hands. The horse must be going forward

with impulsion all the time and keep its collection, and if necessary increase it.

The shoulder-in can also be ridden on a circle. Shoulder-in through the corner is a very difficult exercise, and should not be practised too early on. Horse and rider have to be ready for this. The tempo is slowed down. The horse is mainly on the outside rein. The inside lower leg pushes the hindquarters on to a larger circle, then the fore-legs describe it. When through the corner the pressure of the inside lower leg is reduced, while the pressure of the outside lower leg is increased and keeps the horse on the circle. The horse has to be kept going forward with neck and head high. When finishing the shoulder-in make the horse go on one track. It should keep the flexion in the neck, then straighten it and ride forward at a lively pace.

Variations for practising the shoulder-in. **1** *Out of the corner into a volte.* **2** *The exercise is repeated in the volte.* **3** *Shoulder-in from the long side into a circle.* **4** *Enlarging the circle while riding shoulder-in.* **5** *Shoulder-in after the corner on the long side, then straight on.*

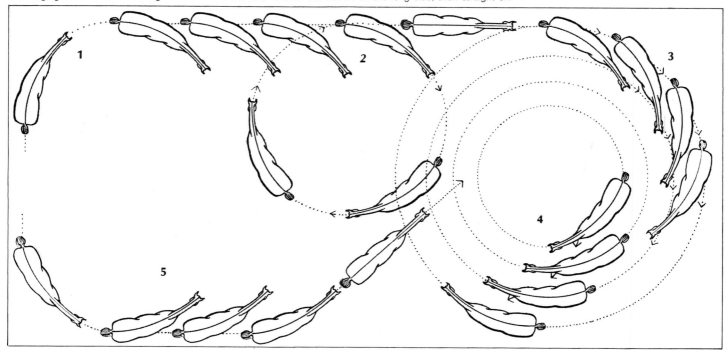

Shoulder-in along the long side correctly ridden, as in a test, with the fore-legs approximately one and a half hoofs' width inside the step of the inner hind-leg. Use a little more angle in the shoulder-in than there would be in the classical shoulder-in, as shown in the sketch on top right.

The rider is sitting evenly on both seat-bones in the middle of the saddle and looking the way he is going. The inside lower leg, which is on the saddle, makes the horse go forward and sideways supported by the inside rein which gives the horse the flexion and retains it. The outside lower leg, behind the girth, maintains the position and must perhaps be brought forward a little together with the giving of the inner rein, if the horse loses balance and angle. The outside rein supports the lower leg, guides the horse in the direction you want it to go and regulates the angle and flexion.

Travers

The horse is bent in body and neck in the direction it is going when ridden in travers. The fore-legs should be on the track while the hind-legs are off the track. Travers is ridden in collected walk or trot.

The horse is put into a travers position after a half-halt. The forehand continues on the track, while the hind-legs are pushed off it with a strong outside lower leg while the rein is holding, so that it will bend its body round the inside lower leg and the hind-legs will stay off the track.

Travers is easiest developed from shoulder-in, and it gradually progresses from there. The inside lower leg has the important function of driving the inside hind-leg forward and under the horse's body. This also forces the outside hind-leg to come farther under the body. Travers on the long side, or along the diagonal, can be practised in the following ways. After a carefully ridden volte in a corner the rider gives a half-halt, just before the front legs of the horse come on to the track of the long side. Then the horse is made to go sideways with strong outside lower leg and inside rein. Both legs make the horse go forward. The reins are in firm contact to keep the collection. The inside lower leg on or just behind the girth controls the horse. This is supported by the inside rein, which positions the horse and keeps it going in the right direction. The outside lower leg farther back makes the horse go sideways, and is supported by the outside rein, which also positions the horse and keeps it from changing angle.

The rider's weight should be slightly more on the inside seat-bone but must not collapse in the hips. Follow the movements smoothly while looking where you are going.

The lateral movements are essentially produced through the outside lower leg and leading inside rein. If the horse is tense or unwilling to do the lateral work it is best to go back to leg-yielding so that it will relax and give. It might be a good idea for the rider to start practising travers after a half-volte or out of the corner as the horse is bent as in shoulder-in. The rider's aids in these movements are the same as for the travers. Travers can also be ridden when making the circle smaller, so that the rider can leave the aids and familiarize himself with, and get the feeling of, the movements. When riding travers on a curved line, the forehand is on the outside track and the hind-legs on the inner, or vice versa (see 5 and 6). It is important that the horse does not lose the angle and fall on its shoulder. When a greater degree of collection has been achieved the rider must watch that the horse keeps an even rhythm and cadence of steps. To finish the travers movement the hind-legs are brought on to the same track as the forehand with the inside lower leg, then straightened and ridden forward.

Changes of the exercises

These are made partly to limber up the horse, to collect it and to make it pay attention. The rider also practises riding with greater precision, using the aids

Variations for practising Travers. **1** *Out of the half-volte. Watch the change of bend when getting back on to the track.* **2** *Along the diagonal after carefully going through the corner.* **3** *Along the long side.* **4** *Travers through riding in decreasing circles.* **5** *Travers on the circle with the hind-leg to the outside.* **6** *Travers with the forehand inside the track of the hind-leg.*

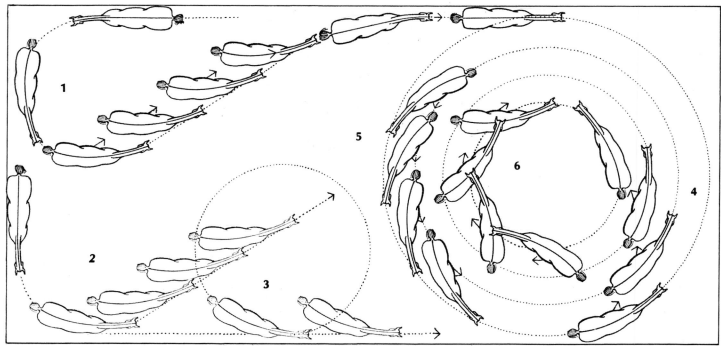

Travers: The rider puts more weight on her inside seat-bone and follows the movement of the horse. The horse is bent around the inside lower leg, which asks the horse to go forward and under. The outside crossing hind-leg is thereby forced to come across. The outside lower leg is behind the girth, and pushes the horse sideways. The outside rein supports the leg and stops the horse from going on its forehand and losing angle. See how horse and rider are looking where they are going, and how well the outside fore-leg is crossing.

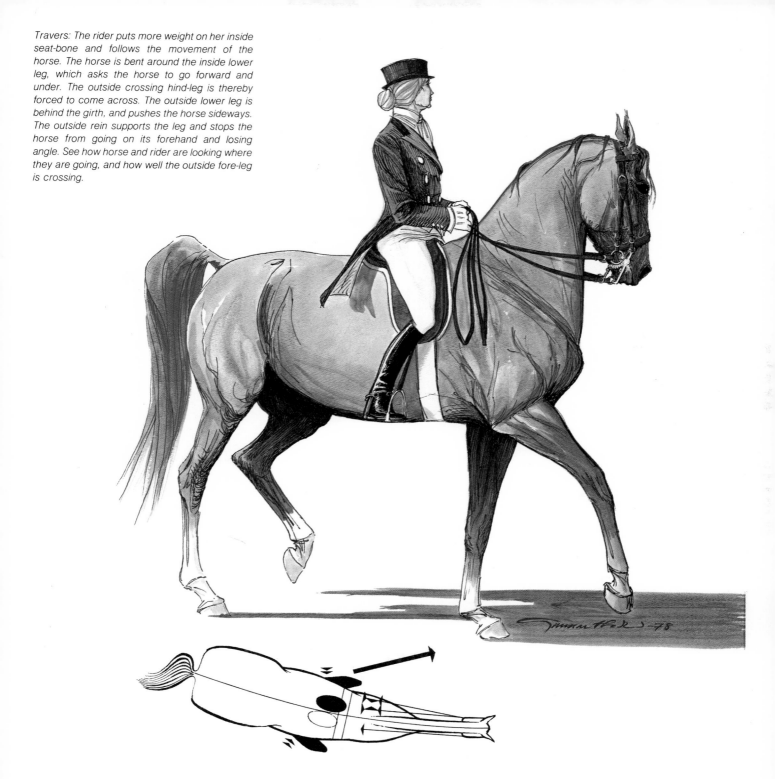

correctly and trying to reach a closer understanding with his horse. The horse should always be ridden on a straight line before changing from one exercise to another. Only when it does exactly what the rider is asking for can these transitions be made correctly. It is important to vary the number of steps in the different exercises, and go straight now and then to keep the attention of the horse and its willingness to go forward. The transitions should be smooth and the collection increased.

1 *Transition from travers to shoulder-in. The horse keeps its bend and is ridden forward in a simple turn. It is given a half-halt when at* **X**, *then ridden in shoulder-in.*

2 *Transition from shoulder-in to travers. The fore-hand is moved on to the track and straightened after a half-halt. The leading outside rein keeps the horse's flexion and position. Then follows the pushing over of the hind-legs with the outside lower leg.*

3 *Transition from shoulder-in to travers through a circle. After riding shoulder-in, it does a small volte, and out of the volte, after a half-halt at* **X**, *does travers.*

4 *Transition from shoulder-in to travers. After a half-halt at* **X** *the rider changes the horse's flexion and changes the position of the leg. This demands softness and suppleness of the rider.*

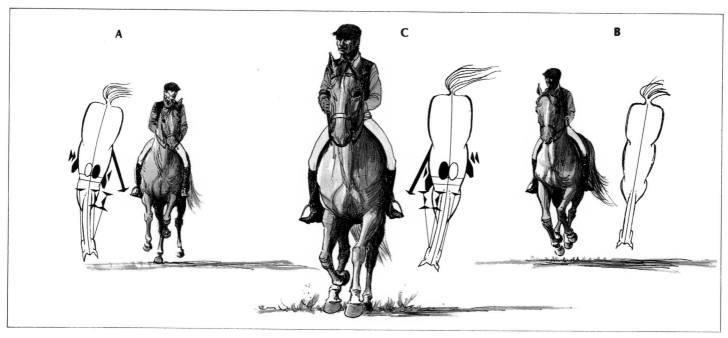

A *Half-pass in canter left. Look at the aids of the rider.* B *Flying change from right to left. Watch the horse is quite straight.* C *Half-pass to right. Look how little bend the horse has got.*

Half-passes to left and right of the centre line

This movement is asked for in the Grand Prix Test and is described as follows: Down the centre line five counter-changes of hand at half-pass to either side of the centre line with change of leg at each change of direction. The first half-pass to the left and the last to the right of three strides, the four others of six strides. Finish on the right leg. (*Compare with the exercises on pages 58-9.*) The judge watches for the angle, the flexion, the softness and obedience, the transition and the correct number of steps. As well as these points, the judge takes into account the lightness and ease of movements, suppleness of back and engagement of hindquarters.

The most difficult thing in the Zig-Zag

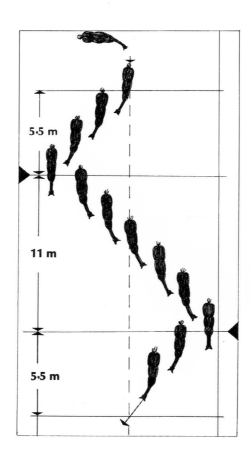

5.5 m

11 m

5.5 m

half-passes is that each half-pass of 11m must be carried out in six strides, and the first and last 5½m in three strides. To make it easier for the rider, it is a good idea to mark the 11m and put stakes where the change should be made. The Zig-Zags are probably mainly wider to begin with, but the important thing is that the horse has the right flexion and is always straight in the transition. The shortening of the canter strides through increased collection is of secondary consideration. When increased collection and steeper angles are demanded the rider must watch that he keeps the three-time canter. The rider must follow the movement of the horse all the time, sit heavier on the inside seat-bone and look in the direction he is going.

Piaffe

This is a very collected trot on the spot with short but pronounced movements of suspension. The legs should be lifted with increased cadence and in a faster rhythm. The hocks must be well bent and under the horse's body, with the hindquarters lowered and a strong active back. The horse must be completely relaxed in neck, with nose and head nearly vertical and with only a light rein contact (*see picture below*).

To put it simply: the horse must be balanced between leg and hand with the poll the highest point.

It takes three years of work with the horse until its muscles in back and hindquarters have developed sufficiently for it to be strong enough for the increased collection that is necessary for the piaffe without overtaxing it. It must be taken for granted that the horse is straight forward going and does not swing from side to side before the piaffe can be taught.

The trainer needs to use his ingenuity and imagination to teach the piaffe, as there is no definite rule to go by. Some talented horses, like musical child geniuses, seem to find it quite natural to do the piaffe and passage as though it were nothing special. Quite apart from the temperament and adaptability of the individual horse, some have longer, rounder, or slower actions, others shorter or quicker ones.

Decarpentry said in his books about piaffe and passage that the rule which was laid down in the old school, and by Baucher, was that the piaffe was taught first, and then with forward driving-aids, the passage. In contrast to this, Fillis and Saint-Phalle started with the passage, then shortened it to the piaffe (without doubt either method can be effective if carried out by a really experienced rider).

The fore-leg is lifted to roughly the middle of the cannon-bone of the supporting leg and the hind-leg just above the fetlock of the supporting leg.

Halt. Trot. Increased shortening of trot to halt is the way to the piaffe.

Work in hand

The horse should have a snaffle-bit, cavesson, side-reins and lunge-line. The trainer stands behind the shoulder of the horse, roughly the distance of a dressage whip away, but near enough so that he can touch the horse's hind-legs. The person holding the lunge-line keeps it as loosely as possible, so that the horse accepts it confidently.

The horse should first walk, then be made to take a few trotting steps with the help of the whip and voice. The trotting steps are gradually shortened with a firmer hold on the lunge and stronger whip and voice (clicking) until the horse starts to piaffe. The horse must be kept straight, with the forehand and hind-legs on the same track. In order that the horse should not lose the willingness to go forward, it should be allowed to move forward a little. Work with a fresh horse for short periods.

When the horse has accepted and willingly obeys the aids, and carries out the work asked for, it is the time for the trainer to carry on alone (*see picture on right*). He only uses the snaffle and dressage whip. He holds the reins in one hand on the withers. The inside rein should be running under the little finger through the index and middle finger, the outside rein between index finger and thumb. The whip gently touches the hind-leg at the back, and he encourages the horse with his voice (clicking).

Work with the rider

This can start when the horse really lifts his legs. One uses again the cavesson with side-reins and lunge-line. The rider should be positive, and sit into the motions of the piaffe without holding the reins. When the horse has got used to the rider's weight the cavesson and side-reins can be removed.

The rider should have a very light contact with the reins. Legs and back give alternate aids to gradually shorten the trot until the horse does a few piaffe steps. Praise it as soon as it has progressed.

The seat of the rider should be soft and relaxed all the time but firm in the hips, and with a little more weight on the stirrups than in the saddle so as not to interfere with the horse's hindquarters.

The horse is worked in the snaffle with the aid of a long dressage whip. Work along a supporting wall, as it is easier to keep the horse straight.

Work between the pillars

This is used to increase the balance, rhythm and energy of the steps. The goal is to reach the highest degree of collection. To teach the horse levade and other airs above the ground, the pillars are absolutely necessary. The horse has to be able to do the piaffe in hand before it can be put between the pillars, and it must be quiet and accept the work without resistance. The tack needed for this work is snaffle, cavesson, side-reins and straps to attach to the pillars. The straps are fixed to the side-rings of the cavesson and then to the rings on the pillars about 10 to 20cm lower than the wither (higher as collection increases). The shoulders should be in line with the pillars. The horse has first to be taught the limits of movement and get used to being tied in. The trainer stands in front of it to begin with, and moves it gently backward and forward. A helper then holds the horse with a lunge-line fixed to the middle of the cavesson. The trainer, who is now at the side of the horse, puts his hand on its quarters and pushes it gently sideways, first to one side and then to the other, until it moves quietly from one side to the other without worrying.

The next step is to work the horse sideways in the pillars. The whip is used on the outside of the hock. Slowly the horse should move the outside hind-leg forward, but not over the inside leg, which moves forward at the same time that the outside hind-leg is put on the ground. The horse should not stand with straight hind-legs. The assistant keeps the horse straight in front with the lunge-line.

When it is able to do the sideways movements quietly and attentively the trainer can go on working the piaffe. The horse should work in the middle of the two pillars, and must not go directly from the sideways movements into the piaffe. This could cause it to be wide behind and swing. The whip helps to get the hind-legs to be lifted higher, by moving it up and down. To get the horse to lower its hindquarters, it can be touched lightly on the loins. Gradually the horse can be worked with rider and the various 'aids' removed.

Between the pillars. The horse has progressed to the stage when the trainer can work from behind with the pillar whip.

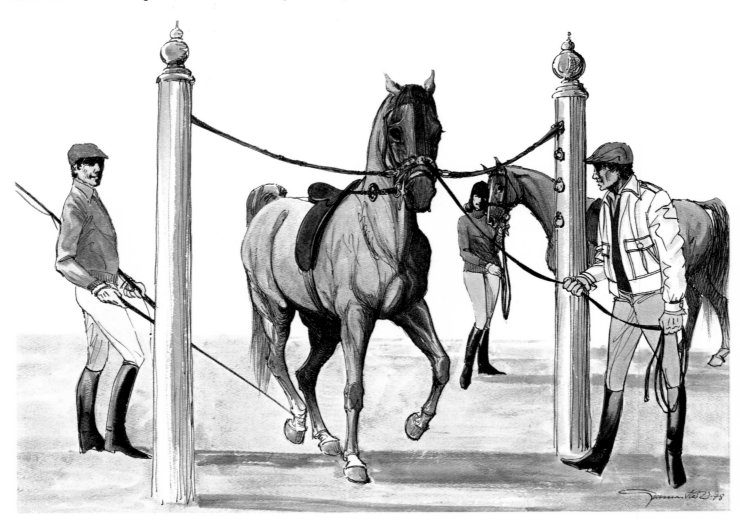

Examine the movements carefully

During further work in the piaffe, ask a knowledgeable rider to watch you and take a ciné film so that you can see exactly what is happening. It should look as shown in the picture top right. The horse should have moments of suspension: the quarters truly lowered, the fetlock of the leg on the ground, flexed, the other hind-leg lifted well above the supporting one. Hoof and fetlock are suspended. The supporting fore-leg must be straight down from the shoulder, and also lowered in the fetlock. The other fore-leg is lifted well above the ground to about the middle between knee and fetlock of the supporting leg. The steps should be on the spot.

The horse must be up in front with a good flexion in the neck, the poll the highest point and the nose vertical. The horse is light in the hand. The seat of the rider must be relaxed, and he must sit light in the saddle in order not to interfere with the increased strain on the horse's back.

Below: **1** *Correct piaffe (compare with picture above)* **2**, **3** *and* **4** *are incorrect variations of the movement.* **2** *The hind-leg not lowered, the hind-legs not sufficiently under the body, the fore-leg tense. The horse is over bent and the rider sits too heavily in the saddle, with legs too far forward.* **3** *The horse is almost sitting on its hocks. It is too low in front. The rider is sitting too far forward, and has lost contact with the horse's*

mouth. The swishing of the tail indicates the resistance and discomfort of the horse. **4** *The hind-legs hardly leave the ground. The horse is not collected. The rider is rough with his hands, and tries to pull the horse together with too strong a leg and hands too high as well as body too far back, which interferes with the horse's action. The horse has a 'broken neck'. Ears and tail show resistance and discomfort.*

Above: Piaffe as near as possible perfect, although a single picture cannot show whether the actual movements are correct. The horse steps with good flexion in its joints. Well-lowered hindquarters. The legs are lifted to the correct height, and the position of neck and head is right. The rider is relaxed, and sits light in the saddle.

Passage

This is slow, collected trot with high, vigorous, rhythmic and even steps with cadence and a definite suspension. The picture on the right shows how it should look. The fore-leg should be lifted to the height of the middle of the cannon-bone of the supporting leg. The hind-leg should be lifted so that the hoof reaches first above the fetlock of the supporting hind-leg. The hind-leg should have spring in the steps and come well under. The fetlock of the supporting legs should be supple so that the horse can keep the suspension.

The horse must be straight and relaxed and have a light contact with the reins, be up in front and 'give' in its neck, with head and nose vertical. It depends to some extent on the conformation of the horse and its temperament how it will carry out this movement, whether it will be lively or slow. In their natural surroundings many horses show an inclination to go in a passage-type of trot in certain situations. For example, the pleasure a stallion shows in a mare is often displayed in this way, and the same applies to a new arrival showing off to the other horses in the field, or a horse that is being led back to the stable when the feed is waiting for it. In the passage-like trot the horse moves with high rhythmic, regular diagonal steps with marked cadence and movement of suspension but without any collection, and completely relaxed. The rider who uses too strong a hand and not enough leg, who tries to collect the horse just with the hand, can get a passage-type trot. The horse leans on the hand, pushes with the hind-legs as it cannot go forward because of the hard hands, but does not bend in the neck and goes above the bit. It does move up and down, and the rider gets the impression of doing passage.

To do passage the horse must have reached a high degree of collection, be straight and not tense. The classical way to teach passage is through the piaffe, but one will not be able to get passage by making the horse go forward out of the piaffe. The horse has to learn to keep the cadence even when moving forward; it must be balanced and light in the hand. Too slow a pace when teaching makes it too difficult for the horse to use its hind-legs energetically.

One can make a transition from the extended trot to the collected, and try to keep the activity of the hind-legs in a more condensed form, and more under the body. The forward movement is reduced, and the horse is light in the hand. A helper can use a long whip to make the hind-legs go under the body. The rider gives small, rhythmic half-halts, collects the horse with his legs to keep the diagonal springy steps.

If the helper touches the fore-leg with the whip at the moment the horse lifts the leg, this will make it lift it higher. In doing so it rests longer on the other leg.

The rider uses a stronger leg to move a few metres in passage from the piaffe.

Passage: **A** *The horse rests in trot with lowered fetlocks and with the diagonal legs lifted high. The supporting legs are then stretched so that the moment of suspension* **B** *is increased* **C**. *The horse puts down the other diagonal legs, keeps the suspension long enough with all four legs to be able to bend the fore-leg so that the lower leg is almost vertical with the ground.*

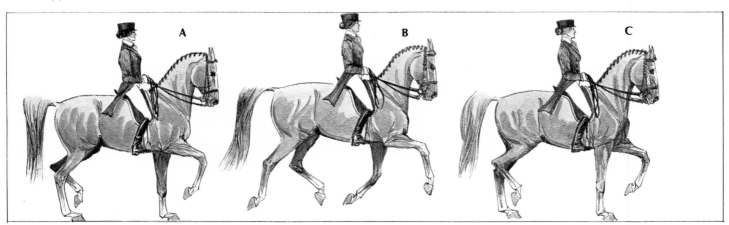

A   B   C

Fore- and hind-legs should be lifted with great energy, the point of the hoof of the fore-leg as far as the middle of the cannon-bone of the leg on the ground. The point of the hoof of the hind-leg points towards the fetlock of the resting hind-leg. The horse should be well up in front with 'give' in the neck, the poll the highest point and the head vertical with the ground. There should be only a light contact with the reins, the horse carrying itself.

The horse keeps the suspension for a few steps, but cannot stay in balance for long. It has to be pushed forward in collected trot to regain balance and come light in the hand. Piaffe from the collected trot with cadence is repeated until the horse can move directly from piaffe into passage.

It is hard work for the horse to learn piaffe and passage, physically as well as mentally, and should not be practised every day, and not more than 40 to 45 metres. Great concentration is also demanded of the rider. So change the routine and go out for a hack, and perhaps have a few jumps. Use the horse's homeward instinct to practise and make the work easier.

Jumping

The saying is that the important thing is 'to go well, not to win'. Where jumping is concerned one should realize that competitions are not won over the fences, but between the fences. It is then that the rider can give the horse a chance to jump the fences cleanly. It is between the fences that the seconds are saved.

When jumping a course, horse and rider have to be of the same mind to give their best in the short time. They have to take risks, perhaps, but in the end they ride better and faster than the other competitors.

The essential ingredient for this is not only the physical ability of the horse but its courage and absolute confidence in its rider. This can only be built up slowly — strength through fitness training — ability and willingness gradually developed by the rider through his really getting to know the horse and never asking the impossible.

Ability and touch go hand in hand. The ability to judge distances and ground conditions, combined with knowing the horse's ability and fitness, is usually the deciding factor in the result. That is jumping!

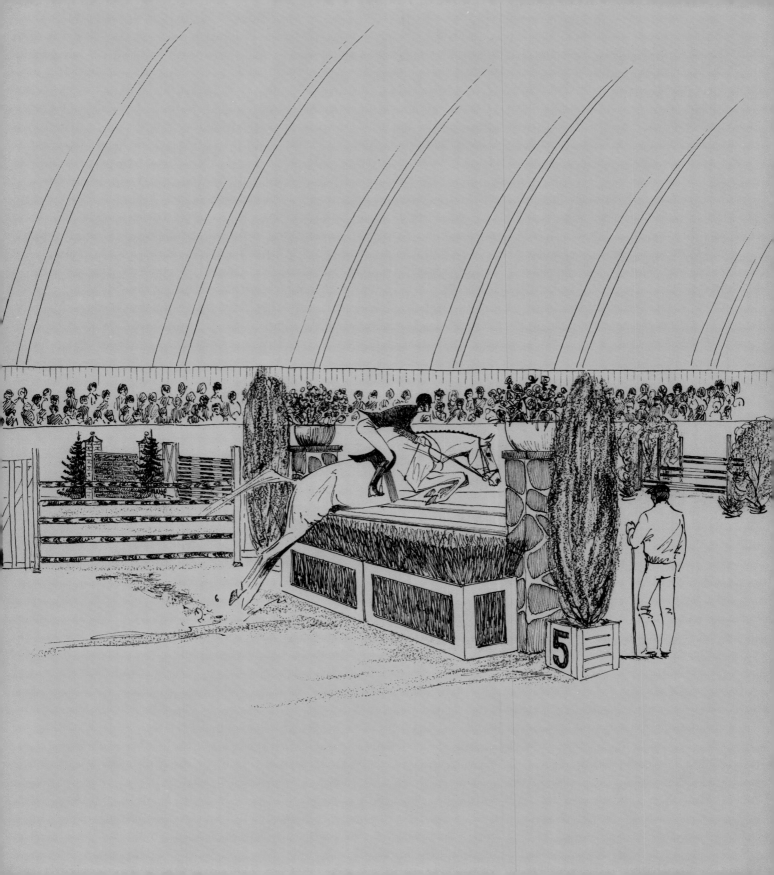

The horse is collected and ready to approach the jump.

Controlled explosion—the show-jumper

Jumpers should be straight, quiet and forward-going as well as sensible. The 'explosion' must be clearly visible but the horse must not 'explode' before the rider gives his permission. The show-jumper should be a sort of 'controlled explosion'.

The horse should be built to take the strain

They must be strong, have good bone, flat joints, relatively short cannon-bones and well-formed pasterns. There should be room between the jawbone and the

neck to allow flexion at the poll, and the neck well put on in proportion to the rest of the body. Furthermore, the jumper should have a definite wither with strong, firm muscles to put the saddle into the correct position, a long, sloping shoulder, a deep chest with rounded ribs. The ideal is a back that is not too straight, neither too long nor too short, and strong hindquarters.

The show-jumper must enjoy show-jumping, it has to be courageous and free-moving. Its most important pace should be the canter, and in this it ought to be able to take long strides and always be controllable. It has to be able to shorten or lengthen the stride, slow down, or speed up and react quickly.

Forward seat or upright seat?

The upright seat makes it easier for the rider to influence his horse, to push on a timid one, to collect the horse that pulls too much, and to balance it better. The forward seat takes the rider's weight off the horse's back, and does not interfere with its action. It is easier for the rider to follow its movements in this position (*see page 26*).

The rider knows best when to use either one or the other of these seats to make things easier for his horse.

The hands should always be quiet hands. Hands all over the place worry the horse as well as the spectators. Still hands that give the aids quietly yet definitely at the right moment will achieve the best results.

The difference between the positions of the lower leg in the forward seat depends to some degree on the build of the horse and the rider. Study as many riders and horses as possible.

The stirrup leathers must be fixed in such a way that the thigh can move easily, yet be on the horse, so that the rider has full control without interfering with its freedom of movement. The middle of the lower leg, between the knee and just above the heel, pushes the horse forward. The heel and spurs collect.

The reins should be as long as possible, but the rider must be able to control the speed and direction without being left behind.

The hands act like a spring that controls the reins; giving and taking, keeping a light contact with the horse's mouth.

The trick is to ride the properly prepared horse in all situations quietly and under control, and to ask no more of the horse than it is ready to jump — not too high or too wide — and not to go too fast, so that it can cope within its limits of training and ability.

The rider who relies on brute force, just pushing his horse on without control of speed, with rough hands and legs, has obviously no proper knowledge of the practical or theoretical approach to jumping. It is often more good luck than good management that they manage to stay in the ring and finish — although the result is usually several knock-downs and refusals. Use your head when jumping!

*Below left: A forward seat. **A** Plumb-line. **B** Balance forward in action, the legs supporting, the seat goes with the movement. The hindquarters are free, and the horse can canter easily. Right: The upright seat. The plumb-line is somewhere between **A** and **B** depending on the phase of the canter stride. In the upright seat the horse can be pushed forward with the seat. The reins and stirrups must be longer. Someone who rides a lazy horse should not have his stirrups so short as to make it difficult for him to change between the upright and the forward seat.*

Equipment for the show-jumper

The most important thing is that the saddle fits. It should rest on the muscles that run on either side of the backbone. When it is put on the horse without a numnah one should be able to look through the channel of the saddle from the cantle to the pommel. The pommel of a jumping saddle should be relatively high and the flaps thicker and the lowest seat point of the saddle a little in front of the middle.

The quality of the leather and workmanship should be first-class. The rider must make certain that the leather, the seams, the girth and stirrup leathers are in perfect condition and up to the stresses which occur when jumping.

The choice of numnah depends on the sensitivity of the horse. Remember that some synthetic fibres can burn and chafe. This also applies to girths made of nylon or Terylene. The best girths are made of webbing. Check the girth regularly. It can happen that when a horse makes an extra effort over a jump the girth or the girth buckles break. A cheap life insurance is to use a surcingle in training and at shows (*see picture below*). A breast-plate helps to keep the saddle in position. This can be lined with sheepskin to make it comfortable.

Do not experiment unnecessarily with different bits, and side or other reins that restrict the horse. If the horse chews too much on the bit it might help to alter the position of it in its mouth. As the jumper turns with the rein-aids, a snaffle with checks might be useful. This cannot slip through the mouth or hurt it at its corners. It is also easier to keep clean than an ordinary snaffle with

The show-jumper below is equipped with the following: A well-fitting saddle, numnah, surcingle, breast-plate, snaffle, drop noseband, bandages, overreach boots, brushing boots.

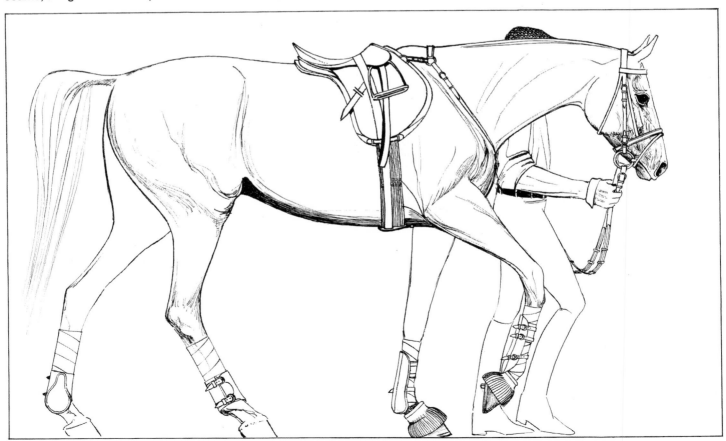

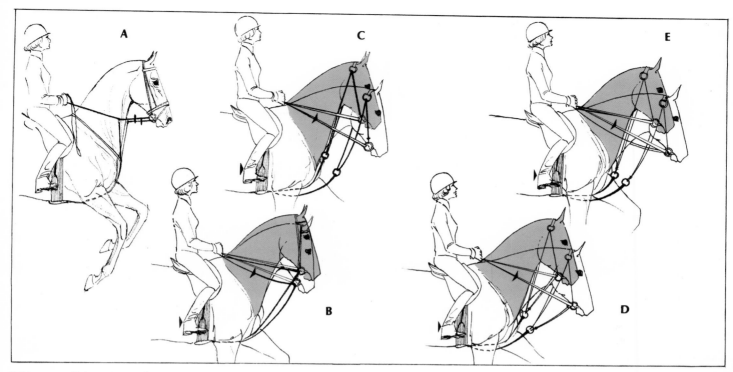

A *Martingale* B *Running-rein* C *Chambon* D *Independent Gogue* E *Fixed Gogue.*

rubber bit-guards. The most important thing is that the bit is clean and has no sharp edges.

The noseband is chosen according to the horse's needs, either an ordinary noseband, drop noseband, Grackle or Flash. Cotton reins with leather stops are most suitable, as they are easier to keep hold of and are not slippery when wet. Many horses need boots. They are easier to put on than bandages. Be careful that gravel or sand does not lodge under them and rub and cause an infection.

Martingales

These are not put on to pull the horse together. They are only an effective help when the rider works the horse from behind. The most usual, simplest and at the same time mildest one is an ordinary running martingale (**A**). It prevents the horse from throwing up its head, and at the same time helps to guide the reins. It must not be put on too short.

The running rein (**B**) helps the horse to keep its head in the right position. It helps the collection only when the rider uses a strong leg to ride the horse into it, and secondly when the horse's head is forward and not too high. The rider then relaxes the rein and the horse takes a light contact with the snaffle. The more the horse's hindquarters are engaged, the more the centre of gravity is moved back and the head and neck are carried in the correct position.

If the running rein is used incorrectly so that the horse's head is pulled too low it causes strain on the neck, shoulder and back muscles. The horse does not engage its hindquarters and goes on the forehand with the wrong bend in the neck.

The chambon **C** (*see also pages 22-3*) acts with a slight pressure behind the

ears on the poll. If the horse throws up its head the bit moves high up in its mouth, but as soon as it drops its head the bit drops back into its normal position. Here also the rider has to ride the horse forward.

The Gogue

There are two types of this, the independent and the fixed Gogue. The independent Gogue (**D**) looks like the chambon but acts more or less like the running rein. The pressure is also just behind the ears of the horse but has a wider distribution. Some of the direct contact with the horse's mouth disappears.

The fixed Gogue (**E**) is used together with the normal rein and has the same effect as the bridoon. When the horse drops its head and neck the Gogue is no longer effective and then takes a light contact with the bit. It is necessary to ride the horse forward.

1	2	3	A

The technique of the show-jumper

Supple back and balance. Balance is as important for the jumper as it is for the dressage horse.

The jumper is perhaps even more collected just before the jump than the Lipizzaner when executing a levade (*see picture below*). Freedom of movement followed by collected work is the be-all and end-all. The way the horse then jumps a fence depends on the neck and balance reflexes (*see page 10*).

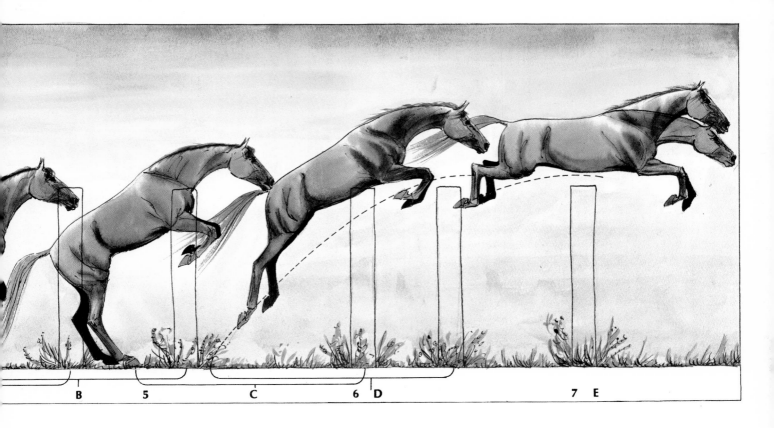

B   5   C   6   D   7   E

1 The last canter stride on approaching the jump is completely different from the strides earlier on, which had collection with the hind-legs well under the body. The body is now lowered as the fore-legs stretch out farther.

2 The horse is able to use the fore-legs to a greater effect when the body is lowered, as the muscles are better utilized. Added to this you have the push upward and this is similar to the pole-vault, where the pole lifts the athlete until the pole is vertical.

3 The lifting stage finishes here. The horse's muscles work harder, and the

Comparison of the Lipizzaner in levade and the jumper at the point of take-off. The black lines show the path of the feet. The curve made by the front feet is not always as steep as that of the hind, as the horse is going forward.

limbs stretch and push upward. The reflexes make the horse lift its head and neck when the fore-legs are stretched out and the hind-legs lowered. The hind-legs come under the body before lifting off the ground and before the fore-legs are bent, so that the body is placed at the correct angle before the jump. When the forehand leaves the ground there is a moment of suspension before the hind-legs are put down.

4 The hind-legs touch the ground now, usually closer together than in a normal canter stride. This varies, depending on the approach.

5 The neck is stretched and rounded. The reflexes make the horse tuck its fore-legs up and push with the stretched hind-legs. This needs great strength.

6 The hind-legs leave the ground and the horse is in the air. The fore-legs

have to be tucked in already at the moment of suspension at 3 and 4 so that the obstacle is not knocked down. They stay in this position until the obstacle is cleared. The hind-legs bend as soon as they leave the ground.

7 When the fore-legs are over the fence they stretch out again in preparation for the landing. Each horse has a special way of using itself while in the air so as not to knock the fence down with its hind-legs. Some tuck them right underneath the body, some sideways, and some kick out. A horse that jumps well arches its back, neck and head in a curve with the wither the highest point when it is over the centre of the jump **E** (Bascule).

A, B, C and **D** show where the legs are in relation to the jump.

85

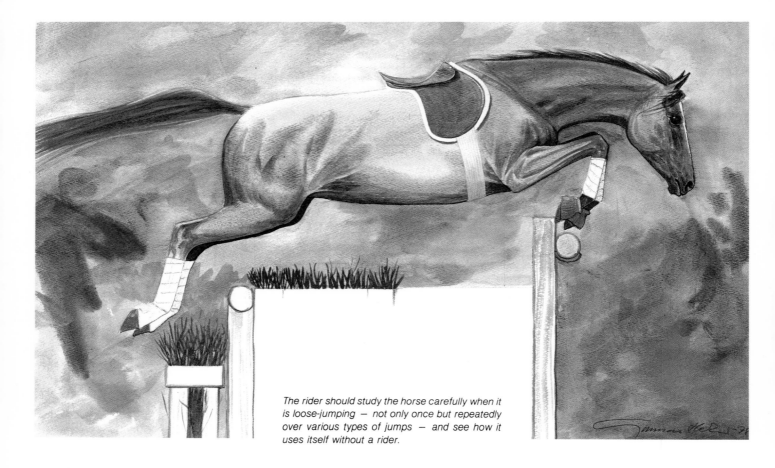

The rider should study the horse carefully when it is loose-jumping — not only once but repeatedly over various types of jumps — and see how it uses itself without a rider.

Loose - jumping

The preparation for jumping is not always carried out as carefully as the flat work. It usually consists of a few cavalletti and some natural fences. Very often the rider has no idea how the horse will behave over the fence; it is frequently worried by the weight on its back and uncertain aids of the rider. Mechanical objects such as cars and aeroplanes are studied, tested and tried before they come into use. The horse should be given a chance to show how it reacts to the various obstacles. It should have the opportunity to develop and gain experience without the rider on its back.

Where jumping is concerned, the rider has to adapt himself to the horse and its movements. When loose-jumping, the horse has the chance to work out for itself its own movement and approach to the jumps. This will give the rider some idea of how it should be ridden over fences.

When loose-jumping it can jump with natural balance and decide for itself where to take off, and at what speed. The rider can help the horse to find the right moment of take-off by the spacing of the fences. A flick of the whip or clicking of the tongue also helps.

A jumping course

By using a wall, a few wings, 10 to 12 cavalletti and perhaps a natural fence it is possible to build a course that is varied. It need not be too expensive, or too complicated. The purchase of some poles, wings, cavalletti, a brush fence and a wall is money well invested.

The following distances must be learned and accurately used when jumping cavalletti in walk, trot or canter.

Normal distances for cavalletti are as follows:

Walk: 1m
Trot: 1·20 to 1·40m
Canter: 3·50 to 5·00m

These distances are reduced by 10 to 20 per cent for ponies.

Vary the distances in the canter from minimum to maximum to make the exercises more difficult for the horse. The picture below gives some idea of the training programme. The exercises must, of course, relate to the stage of the horse's training and its fitness. The horse must enjoy them. On page 88 you will find further jump combinations described in detail.

A *The horse over simple cavalletti.*
B *Landing over a rather short combination.*
C *The combination of jumps is shown at the bottom of the sketches. Above that are shown the last three jumps. The shortening of the distances helps the horse to find the right point of take-off. Here the trainer can help the horse by voice, clicking or a light crack of the whip touching the hocks just before take-off.*

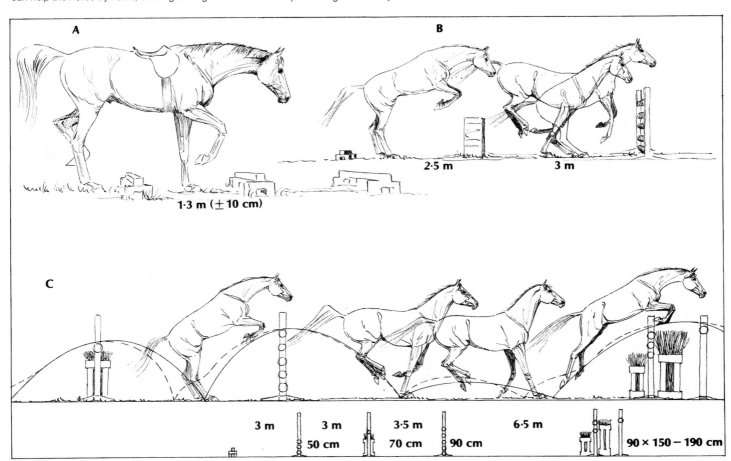

Work over cavalletti

This is the preparation for jumping. It settles the horse and relaxes it. The work over cavalletti is first done in trot. The rider rises at the trot and with the hands tries to follow the horse's movements. A lot of jumps at varying distances create the ground-work. The horse's reflexes are trained and the rider improves his seat. He can do this exercise slowly with hands passive and quiet above the wither, without having contact with the reins.

Cavalletti can also be ridden in sitting trot. The contact between horse and rider is increased, and the horse has to make more use of its back. Gradually horse and rider practise over the combinations in canter (*see diagrams below*). When jumping the rider should feel as though the horse was just doing lengthened and elevated canter strides.

Trotting in rising trot over cavalletti with a completely loose rein.

Suitable cavalletti combinations to be used in canter.

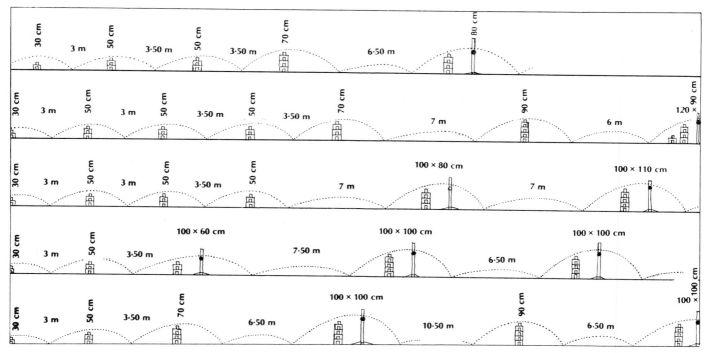

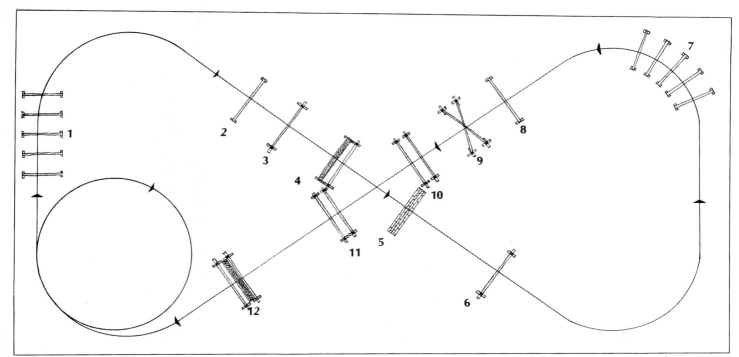

Gymnastics

Above: Course built to be jumped in trot and canter. **1** *(trot) 5 cavalletti distance 1·30m,* **2** *(trot) pole 2·5m to* **3** *(canter) gate 60cm, 3·10m to* **4** *upright 80 × 80cm, 3·00m to* **5** *wall 80cm, 5·5m – 6·00m to* **6** *post and rails 80cm* **7** *(trot) 5 cavalletti on a curve middle distance 1·30m* **8** *pole 2·50m to* **9** *(trot) crossed poles 70cm, 3·00m to* **10** *(canter) upright 80 × 80cm (alternative oxer) 3·00m to* **11** *oxer 90 × 80cm, 6·50m to* **12** *oxer 1 × 1m trot. Repeat. The distances given here are shorter than the normal ones.*

Below: The rider can jump these fences without holding on to the reins, and with his arms at the side of his body. This will help his seat and control. Put a neck strap on the horse so that if the rider should lose his balance he can get hold of it, instead of pulling at the horse's mouth with the reins.

This is the next step. A course to school over can be immensely varied, the only thing it has to have is the correct but differing distances so that the horse can keep its rhythm. The jumps should be low but modelled on an ordinary jumping course. Use wings. The distances in relation to the height and width of the jumps are important. The basic distances in combination jumps are between 7·50m and 10·50m, depending on the width and height of the jumps. A = Brush, B = Oxer, C = Upright, D = Treble. The distances vary as follows:

$$A \left\langle \begin{array}{l} B - 10cm \\ C - 30cm \\ D - 20cm \end{array} \right. \qquad B \left\langle \begin{array}{l} A + 40cm \\ C - 20cm \\ D - 30cm \end{array} \right.$$

$$C \left\langle \begin{array}{l} C + 30cm \\ B + 20cm \\ D - 20cm \end{array} \right. \qquad D \left\langle \begin{array}{l} A + 50cm \\ B + 40cm \\ C + 20cm \end{array} \right.$$

Jumping exercises like these are extremely good for loosening up the horse, as well as for helping the collection. The rider is forced to ride the horse every inch and to adjust the aids.

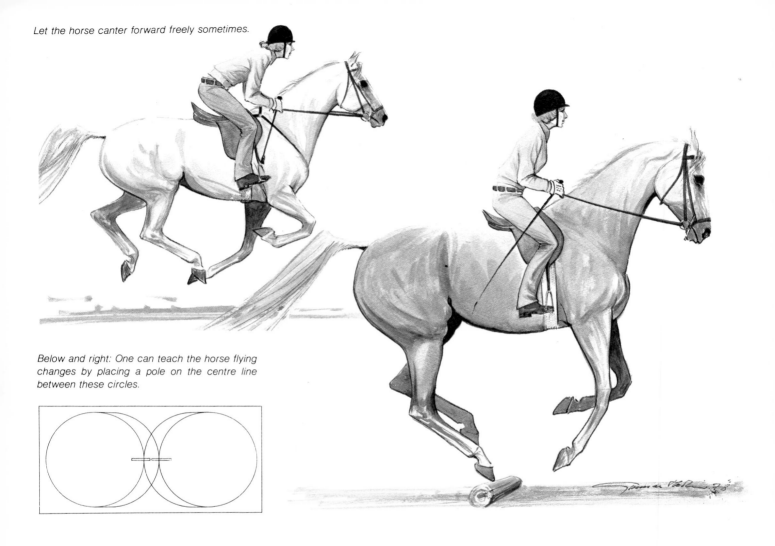

Let the horse canter forward freely sometimes.

Below and right: One can teach the horse flying changes by placing a pole on the centre line between these circles.

Training of the jumper on the flat

Apart from lungeing the horse and loose-jumping it, the training should also consist of the following:
1. Uphill work
2. Cantering and Galloping
3. Cavalletti
4. Jumping
5. Dressage

This could also include driving – which strengthens the shoulder and hindquarters – and swimming – which strengthens all muscles without over-taxing them and improves the breathing.

The aim of the training on the flat is: A To strengthen the horse. B To make it obedient. C To improve its balance.

A. The strengthening of the horse

This consists of building up the muscles and improving the general condition. The horse must first be loosened up, as it will otherwise develop 'resistance muscles'.

A runner starts to loosen up by jumping up and down, and doing some bending and other gymnastic exercises before starting his running training. At the end of his training period he repeats these exercises as well as being given a massage. The principle is the same for the jumper. It does not pay to go rushing up a hill at a fast trot to strengthen back and hindquarters. Start slowly in walk, on a long rein. Let the horse be able to stretch its neck. Let it trot over different

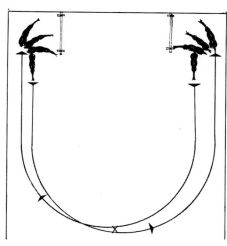

Teach the horse a half-pirouette by riding it into a restricted corner. The horse will be handier as a result on the course.

types of ground, to improve its awareness, canter when the going is good and intersperse with walk periods. Walk up and down hills. Start with five minutes and gradually increase the walk and trot periods on the way home. The horse's homeward urge can be used to ride it in a very collected canter.

The total time spent on the exercises described should be about 45 and 75 minutes. The horse should enjoy this work and be relaxed.

This training is varied and supplemented with cavalletti work and jumping. It loosens the horse as well as collecting it. Interspersed with this can also be prolonged canters alternating with short bursts at gallop, the whole lasting 10 to 20 minutes. It is important to take into account the horse's age, its fitness and the state of the going.

B. To make the horse obedient

This simply means dressage. The horse is not only made supple but also collected. To make a good event horse its dressage must be up to at least medium standard, including half-passes and flying changes.

The lateral work automatically collects the horse, turns on the haunches in all paces, bends the joints and makes it handy. If the horse can do a half-pirouette it does not need a lot of room to turn (see picture above). Balance and safety in jumping are improved if the horse can do flying changes. The horse can be taught these out of a circle over a pole (see picture on page 90). Ride the horse in a circle. When changing the circle the horse has to cross over a pole on the ground or a cavalletti which lies

on the centre line (see diagram page 90). The rider gives the aids for a flying change just before the pole and changes the bend. This should be done at a good working pace. The pole helps the horse to change, and makes it easier.

C. To balance the horse

When the horse's back and hindquarters have been strengthened through training, and it is obedient to the rider's forward and restraining aids, it is time to ask for a more supple and active back to balance it properly. Be in control of the shoulder and you are in control of the hindquarters. When you have control over the hocks you have control over the horse.

Canter with increased collection

A rounded and active canter is a great advantage when jumping at a show. It must also be possible to exaggerate the collected canter as mentioned before. When collection is increased the centre of gravity is moved backward so that the horse is able to carry its weight more easily. There is more strength in the hind-legs when they start the upward push. The rider should therefore increase the collection in accordance with the difficulties of the jump.

*Above: Normal three-time canter. The horse shown has a high degree of collection. It touches down after the suspension **1** on the right hind-leg **2** left hind-leg and right fore-leg touch down, **3** left fore-leg touches down. When the leading fore-leg (left here) leaves the ground the moment of suspension starts, and finishes when the outside hind-leg (here right) touches the ground again. The sign under each horse shows the shortened stride distances taken.*

Below: Four-time canter. The horse touches down after the moment of suspension with **1** right hind-leg **2** left hind-leg **3** right fore-leg **4** leading left fore-leg. Here also the signs show the forward movement in this phase.

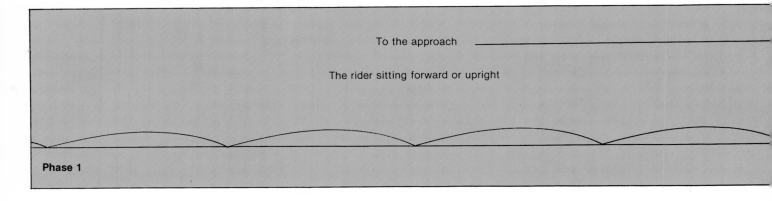

The way to jump

One does not win a jumping competition over the fences but between the fences from the start to finish. This can be divided into three parts. How should the rider behave in each phase?

Phase 1: The Approach
The rider is sitting forward or upright.
A. Determine the approach.
B. Look at the jump and decide what line to take.
C. Decide at what speed to approach the jump.

Phase 2: The approach up to moment of take-off
The rider is sitting forward.
A. Control the approach.
B. Control the direction, look at the fence.
C. Go with the movements.
D. Hands must not pull back.

Phase 3: The take-off
The rider sits forward with seat off the saddle.
A. Control the direction (look behind the jump or at the next one).
B. The rider must not be in front of the horse.

The way to jump starts with the line of approach to the point of take-off in front of the first jump, continues straight away after landing to the next fence, etc. If the time for the course to be jumped is

about 1 minute, the rider rides the horse for about 45 to 50 seconds between the jumps and over the jumps for about 10 seconds. How the horse gets on in those 10 seconds depends on how it is ridden for the other 50 seconds.

But does the show-jumper have to jump with the horse? The answer is 'yes and no'. The rider must follow the horse's movements as closely as possible without interfering with it. The horse should be able to jump as though it did not have a rider on its back. The rider must anticipate the horse's actions so that he can go with the horse when it jumps.

It is important for the rider not to sit in the saddle when in the air. A jump over a fence that is 80 to 90cm high is really only a lengthened canter stride. If the rider is really with the horse over a small jump there should be no difficulties when the fences are raised to 1·40 to 1·50m.

It is not the jump itself that is difficult. The difficulty is not to anticipate trouble and to learn to ride the horse confidently towards the jump. To be frightened is no disgrace. If one admits to being frightened one has made a big step forward. Fright develops through ignorance and insecurity.

When one begins to learn and understand the unknown the nervousness and insecurity disappear.

The way the approach to jumps, and the jumps themselves, is described here is based on Dag Natterquist's theory and teaching. The following is a short and precise description as to how the rider should behave before and over the jump. This applies to novice jumping as well as advanced classes.

The drawing above shows the phases of the approach. The length of the approach can, of course, be shortened or increased, depending partly on how the horse behaves, on the height of the jump, on the going, on what position it is in relation to the other fences, and so on. It may take a long or a short time of encouragement until the horse is confident enough to know how to approach the jump.

'The rider should decide what the horse has to do but give it the freedom to decide how to do it.' (Federico Caprilli).

Phase 1: The Approach
The rider chooses which seat, forward or upright, is the best to keep the horse in balance. The horse must be balanced when approaching the jump.
A. The rider decides the degree of impulsion. The rider has to use legs and voice, perhaps also whip, if the horse does not go forward. It is useless to approach a jump if the horse is not pulling on. The

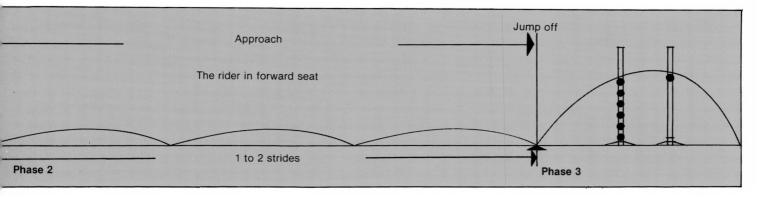

The three phases of the approach to the jump. These are described in detail on pages 98 to 113, and how the rider should behave.

rider has to make the horse go forward and to make it pay attention consistently.

Going forward is the horse's natural inclination. The degree of willingness to go forward varies with different horses. Some pull towards the jump as though it were a magnet, while others are more reluctant and lazy. If the latter is the case, the rider has to use his legs to make the horse go on. If the horse pulls on, perhaps only some slight checks are necessary to keep the right impulsion. A horse that pulls too much must be kept in check so that collection and balance can be achieved.

B. The rider chooses the way to the jump. It is most important that the rider decides as quickly as possible which is the best way to approach the jump, so that he can take the best line and be able to jump over the centre of the fence. The distribution of weight helps to make the horse go the required way as well as leg and rein aids. The rider should keep his eye on the jump the whole time.

C. The speed of approach and impulsion must not be confused. Speed is the tempo at which the horse moves forward. Impulsion creates the movement which the rider uses to reach the right speed. The speed may have to be increased or reduced according to the type, height or width of the jump. The speed should be such that the strides can be shortened or lengthened, whichever is necessary to reach the jump at the correct point of take-off.

Phase 2: The approach to the take-off

The rider sits well forward to take the weight off the horse's back and to interfere with it as little as possible. During the last few strides the horse itself should be able to judge where it should take off and where to shorten or lengthen its strides and so arrive at the right distance for take-off. No rider can ride exactly to the correct point of take-off, although there are top riders who position their horses in such a way that they find the right place for this. When the pair approach the jump the rider must say to his horse 'Well, old pal, I have done my best, now it is up to you.'

A. Rider checks the impulsion. He keeps a firm, steady leg on the horse. The contact with the reins should be light and flexible and not too strong so that the horse feels the rider's hands give and gains confidence to be able to clear the jump.

If the horse is not going forward stronger leg and voice are necessary to get impulsion. The ideal situation is when the rider feels a slight pull towards the jump with his hands passive.

B. The rider controls the direction. Directly towards the middle of the jump the rider makes slight adjustments with the reins if necessary. The horse must not be unsettled with rough and harsh hands that are all over the place. The weight should be well centred, and the legs in continuous contact. The rider should keep his eye on the top of the back pole of the jump, and when near the jump look beyond it to the next.

C. The rider follows the movements. The rider should be as one with his horse to such an extent that the horse hardly feels him on top.

D. The hands must not pull back. The horse must be free to find the point of take-off. The hands, therefore, should be passive in that short moment. The horse must be able to stretch its head and neck as much as it wants to. The wrists should be supple and flexible so that they instinctively keep a light contact with the horse's mouth.

Phase 3: The take-off

The rider sits well forward to give the horse every chance, and not to interfere with it. The jump-off is conditioned by the neck and balance (*see page 10*), which are easily disturbed. The rider should therefore not try to influence the horse but relate to it and follow its movements as much as possible.

A. The rider controls the approach. The rider controls the approach by looking at a point beyond the jump, or if possible at the next jump. If the horse pulls to either one side or the other it must be connected with the reins. The rider must not move his weight about but stay in the centre of the saddle and have equal pressure on both stirrups.

B. The rider must not be in front of the horse. The horse has to jump, not the rider. To be able to follow the horse, the rider has to wait, and as closely as possible co-ordinate his movements with those of the horse. The leg must be in the correct position, the toes slightly turned out so that the heel can be effective in the jump. The upper body swings in rhythm with the horse; how much depends on the jump. Do not throw arms and upper body too far forward, as that could easily disturb the horse and make it knock the fence down. Build up supple and co-ordinating movements and quiet, firm aids when necessary.

Over the jump

The jump itself is the result of the work that went on before. The rider cannot do more than hope that the horse will pick up all its four legs.

Most pictures of jumpers are taken at the moment they are suspended in the air over the jump, as shown in the sketch on page 97. Can something be learned from this picture? Yes, one can study the horse's shape. It uses its back well. The rider follows the jump, is neither left behind nor in front of it. There is no interference with the horse's head or neck; it was able to stretch it as much as it wanted, and the head is lowered so that the wither is the highest point. The slightly open hands and the arms of the rider make an almost straight line from the horse's mouth to the rider's elbow.

The landing

This too, like the take-off, is conditioned by the horse's reflexes. The fore-legs stretch out automatically when head and neck are lifted just before touching down. The fore-legs were rather close together all the time over the jump, but are coming farther apart now, and the outside fore is put down first and takes the full weight of horse and rider. The inside fore follows and takes off some of the weight. Should both legs touch down at the same time there is a great danger that the horse will stumble and fall.

The rider's upper body is first thrown forward and downward and then forward on landing. The rider has to sit against this movement, so as not to make it too difficult for himself or the horse. The upper body should come up with legs close to the horse and a little forward, and feet deep in the stirrup. When the horse moves forward again the rider's upper body should come forward again and the hands give the reins. It is very important to go with the horse when it has touched down and is taking its first rather clumsy canter strides. It makes it easier for it to regain its balance and go actively forward. Only then can the horse resume its normal canter.

The horse jumps with rounded back. The wither is the highest point. The rider goes with the horse. Look at the slightly open hands.

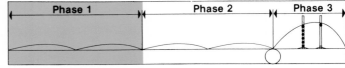

Phase 1	Phase 2	Phase 3

The way to the jump

The rider is sitting forward or upright.
- Determines the impulsion.
- Determines the direction.
- Determines the speed.

The horse is light in the hand and in balance

This is the goal the rider should aim at when riding towards a jump. Try to be in complete accord with your horse. Try to place the horse in such a way that it will find it easy to get over the jump. When jumping at a new show, consider that the horse might find it strange and want extra encouragement and help.

The activity of the hind-legs should be increased right from the start. Ride with concentration and determination towards the first jump. Do not approach it as if it were not important, and just a little practice jump. If the horse refuses

or knocks it down, it can influence both its own and its rider's confidence.

On the forehand

It can make a horse go on its forehand if it knocks a fence down. It pushes off with the fore-legs and the hind-legs follow and it loses its balance completely and feels as though it were on its knees. The rider has to make certain it regains its balance as soon as possible, which sometimes necessitates stronger aids.

A horse that is on its forehand can give the impression of having impulsion and going forward as it canters with quick, short strides. Just as when a person stumbles, he tries to right himself and regain balance through a few short jumps. This does not need a great deal of effort, as the horse pushes with the

hind-legs and thrusts and supports with the fore-legs. The result is that it often puts down its diagonal legs in the wrong order. **1** left hind **2** left fore **3** right hind **4** right (leading) fore (*see picture on page 54*).

A horse that has momentarily 'fallen to pieces' — in other words, is not using its back — does not necessarily go on its forehand, and it is the same with a horse that throws up its head at times. A horse can be on its forehand even if the neck is high and the nose almost vertical. This can be caused by it realizing that it is on its forehand and trying to balance itself again by lifting head and neck.

An experienced and sympathetic rider hardly ever gets into this situation, but it can happen that when the speed is increased the horse loses collection and

Upright or forward seat? It depends on the horse's behaviour, and what the jump looks like. It is the rider who decides which is the most suitable.
Above: Horse on its forehand.
Right: Ready for the jump.

comes on to its forehand. A sympathetic rider realizes straight away when this happens and tries to balance the horse again by keeping a strong hold and very active legs.

It is necessary to have the centre of gravity behind the saddle so that the horse can clear the fence.

The rider should practise the changes of tempo without losing balance. It is necessary for the horse to keep balance and impulsion whether it is going slowly or fast so that it is well within itself, ready for the jump.

Forward or upright seat

This must not be an arbitrary decision. It must not be believed that the forward seat is the one and only one, just because one or more riders have been successful using it. Each horse and rider is individual, and not comparable with others.

Use the seat that suits your horse best, be it upright or forward. If the horse finds it easier to balance and jump if you sit forward — sit forward. It is impossible to lay down hard and fast rules. Each horse is an individual, and reacts differently to given situations and surroundings.

The rider must see that the horse has every chance, when approaching the jump, to be able to jump clear.

The rider should give the horse the opportunity to find the right place for take-off by riding at the correct speed and straight at the jump, correcting if necessary.

'Well, my boy, you are keen, but I decide. Quiet. You must be straight before we jump. I say when. Don't rush so, this is not the Great Wall of China! This small obstacle is like a little hump. Now — I trust you — please!'

This horse is ready and can decide where to take off. The rider has done all he can. The horse is collected. The speed is right. There is plenty of impulsion. The line of approach is correct. The rider watches over the horse's reactions on the approach to the jump.

This horse is not pulling on to the jump. In this situation it is necessary to encourage it. 'Come on, get on with it, you are supposed to jump over the fence, not go under it. You are the one that has to do the jumping. Now, canter, canter.' Clicking, leg, whip if necessary. The horse has to go forward at the right speed. The action must come from behind and there must be a willingness to go forward. The rider must be able to transfer his keenness and energy on to the horse.

Look at the different position of the ears when compared to the horse on page 100. That horse is eager to jump. This one here hesitates, though listening to the rider.

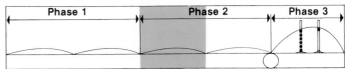

Phase 1	Phase 2	Phase 3

During the approach

The rider in forward seat
- watches the impulsion.
- controls the direction (looks towards the fence).
- goes with the movement.
- hands must not pull back.

Phase 2: Approach to jump-off

This is perhaps the most exciting moment of jumping. The rider leaves the responsibility to the horse and takes over the role of supervisor and controller. This change-over of roles from the one that decides to the one that accompanies means that the rider now tries to follow the horse's movements to such an extent that it hardly feels the rider on its back.

How should the rider behave to make this possible?
- The rider must trust his horse completely.
- The rider must know how the horse moves.

The confidence between horse and rider must be complete. When the rider has full confidence in his horse this faith is transferred to the animal, which in turn trusts the rider — a trust that is built on the knowledge that the latter will not ask more of it than it is able to do.

The psychological security that is felt by horse and rider creates an inner balance which helps to gloss over the odd mistakes. Do not take these too

Horse and rider in the approach. The horse should have found the right place for take-off after one to two strides. It is collected and paying attention, looking towards the jump. The rider gives a little with the reins, but not too much, so that he keeps contact. This rider is still sitting upright, which is not the usual rule. On another horse he would perhaps sit forward. The rider stresses the point that it is necessary to have the horse well between hands and leg to keep it collected.

seriously: laugh about the silly things which you or your horse do at times. A relaxed pair, in a good mood, has a much greater chance than other pairs not so placed.

Study the horse so that you are really able to go with it and practise continually over small fences, with a loose rein, all the time sitting forward.

The horse is on its own and the rider practises his seat and the control of his position. Have the feet firmly in the stirrups, with the lower legs well on the horse. This supports the upper body, which is forward and so balances the rider. The hands can either be on the hips or over the withers, as though they were holding the reins.

The assumption is that the rider has perfect balance so that he can keep the impulsion and keep straight, and if necessary correct it.

The passive hand allows the horse to choose for itself when to take off. The eyes, the thoughts, the legs, the hands of the rider should work like a well co-ordinated team without interfering with the horse in its movements.

Just before the take-off

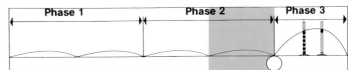

Phase 1 | Phase 2 | Phase 3

Now horse (and rider) have the problem of the jump in front of them. The jump should really be no problem. The pair should be so well trained and familiar with different types of jump that they feel completely confident and approach it as though it were just uneven ground; but watch out — under changed conditions it can look very different. The light can alter things, and when one has had some success one is apt to go for bigger jumps in more advanced classes. The demands on the horse increase, and so does the tension. The whole picture changes, but so gradually that horse

and rider have hardly noticed it. The horse has jumped really well, jump after jump, but suddenly it knocks a fence hard. The rider turns round to see if the fence has been knocked down. 'Why has it knocked this fence down?' 'Oh, here is the biggest fence coming up. Why isn't it going forward?' The horse refuses the next fence.

We must give this some thought. It

should be quite clear to every rider that each jump makes physical as well as psychological demands on the horse. The horse is consistent in all situations, the rider is not. If something unforeseen happens — such as the knocking down of a fence after jumping well — and the horse has gone like clockwork this unsettles the rider and creates too hasty or too slow reactions from him.

I *The hands are passive.*
II *The lower legs are strong, and push so that the hind-legs overtrack the fore-legs. The hands give when the horse wants to stretch its neck to move the fore-legs forward.*

The last stride before take-off. The positions II and III correspond with 2 and 4 above. It might be better to have a forward seat when riding a different horse.

Sometimes these tensions can be so strong that the rider momentarily stops the horse. The tensions transfer themselves straight away to the animal. The rider who should really just follow the horse's rhythm now interferes with it. It reacts straight away and gets unsettled, so that they are not as one any more and refusals are the result. Some people can never become show-jumpers, although they may be good dressage riders and jump well at home, but they have not got the right tempera-

ment. On the other hand, though, there is the rider without nerves; he has to be careful not to be unfeeling towards his horse and demand too much. In either case the horse may refuse. The trust between horse and rider must be complete. During the last few strides and the point of take-off,

- The horse has taken charge
- The rider controls and perhaps corrects the line of approach
- The rider goes with the horse
- The rider must not pull back.

III The lower legs push the hind-legs to the point of take-off, the hands give so that the horse is free in front.

At the moment of take-off. The fore-legs are put down the last time before take-off (also see sketch on right).

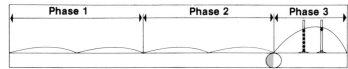

Phase 1	Phase 2	Phase 3

The take-off, first phase

The last counter-stride of the approach forms the first part of the take-off. The fore-legs are put down for the last time before the jump, while the hind-legs touch down for the penultimate time. At this moment the shoulders, head and neck are lowered to a greater or smaller degree, depending on the height of the jump. The higher the jump the lower the body, as the fore-legs have to stretch out more. The projection is increased by the fore-legs being strongly pushed forward. The horse stretches head and neck well forward and the rider has to follow the movement automatically with hands and arms. A supple wrist must be instinctive (but keep contact with the horse's mouth).

A rider who throws his arms and upper body too far forward interferes with his horse.

A horse is greatly helped in the take-off by hind-legs that are well under it, and thereby assist the quick take-off of the fore-legs and shoulders. To regulate the speed of approach is, of course, very important. The more the horse brakes with its fore-legs the higher the forehand will be lifted.

The rider is easily tempted at this moment to come in front of the horse so as not to be left behind. The effect of this is usually that the rider interferes with the rhythm of the horse, which it needs to clear the jump. Either the rider loses complete contact with the horse and jars it on landing, or it is seen that he is in front of the horse and sits back, and thereby gets a nasty jolt on landing. Do not get in front of the horse, wait! —

it is the horse that has to jump, not you. The take-off is instigated by neck and balance reflexes that are very easily disturbed. The rider should therefore try not to influence the horse and concentrate on following its movement as much as he can. The rider has to control the direction. Do this with the reins, but sit still. The slightest shifting of weight influences the horse. The lower leg should be still, with the toes turned out so that the heels can kick and make the horse go forward.

Watch out for the following on take-off:
- Sit quietly in the middle of the saddle.
- Be soft and supple with your hands and arms.
- Never get in front of the horse's movements.

The next section shows the second phase of the take-off.

Tilting

A very sympathetic rider can perhaps influence his horse and improve its jump by using a tilting technique. What is being asked for is stronger action of the fore-legs and an explosive push of the hind-legs. It is only recently that this could be studied with the help of high-speed cameras. This tilting aid has to be given at just the right moment; if the horse is influenced either too early or too late it will not jump well.

The principle is that when jumping a big fence the horse uses its legs, rather as a pole-vaulter uses his pole. Its weight is on the forehand, and the shoulder muscles act like the arms of the pole-vaulter and push forward and up. The short moment is conditioned by a reflex. When the horse's head reaches a more horizontal position the fore-legs are pulled up, and at the same moment the hind-legs stretched. If the rider, at the same moment when the fore-legs are stretched, sits quietly (I) and keeps hold (II) and gives (III) when the fore-legs come off the ground, that has a tilting effect. Only a rider who is well attuned to his horse can achieve this.

The take-off, second phase

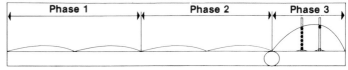

| Phase 1 | Phase 2 | Phase 3 |

This starts when the hind-legs are on the ground and the forehand lifts (Elevation). Neck and nose are raised during the first part of the take-off. Towards the end of this the horse starts to bring its nose forward (*see pictures at bottom of page 107, I phase*). In the second phase the horse arches and pulls in neck and nose (*see II phase on page 107*). When the hind-legs start to stretch they push upward, and the forehead is lifted at the correct angle. Neck and nose stretch out again (*see top left*) to go forward and up when the hind-legs are fully stretched out (*see top of page 109*). Now the horse starts to arch.

The rider must most certainly not interfere with the horse while its head and neck move forward and up, then back, then forward again. A rider who is in front of the horse while the head moves, as above, has no influence over the horse at all. He has no contact with the reins, the hands of the rider are stretched out already and the horse gets a jerk in the mouth.

The rider's hands must first go back with a light contact and straight away afterwards go forward so that there is a constant contact with the horse's mouth. The picture sequences on pages 102-13 show clearly what the rider's position should be.

The joints of the horse's hind-legs function rather like a spring that is compressed and released. It is partly strength, partly the muscles in the hindquarters and thigh and back, that aid this 'spring'. It is the strength in the push-off that determines how high and how wide the horse can jump. The second phase of the take-off is finished when the hind-legs leave the ground.

Here is the 'explosion'.

Elevation angle

The centre of gravity describes a curve in the take-off which is governed − A. Speed, B. Strength of muscles, C. Angle. This angle equals the centre of gravity of the pair. (*See sketch below right.*) The horse has to adjust the angle to suit each jump, and the rider to make sure that the speed is right to give the horse every chance to get over the jump. (*See pages 114-23.*)

An angle of 50° to the ground yields the maximum length of jump. If the strength on take-off is increased, the height and length of the jump will be correspondingly increased. Larger or small angles will make the jump shorter; smaller angle and faster speed will create a longer jump. If the angle and strength are increased the jump will be higher but not longer.

When the rider shifts his weight (which is about 15 to 20 per cent of the total) he makes it difficult for the horse to get over the jump. All these factors have to be taken into consideration, especially over higher and more difficult jumps.

A

Moment of suspension over the obstacle

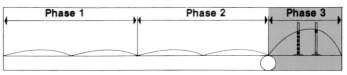

Phase 1	Phase 2	Phase 3

The horse should jump the same way with the rider on its back as it does when it is loose-jumping — that is, with a well-arched back, long, low neck and nose forward. In the bigger classes nearly all horses jump with an active back. The horse that jumps over the bigger fences with a hollow back would be more successful, safer and more pleasant to ride if it did use its back more. If, when the horse is in the air over the jump, it does not have the same outline as it did when loose-jumping, it is the rider's fault and that of earlier training. A rider who is self-critical is not satisfied just to get over the jump.

The sketches above show how the rider should sit, with the heels down all the time and the knees and lower legs in the same position while over the jump. If the heels come up, so do the knees, and the balance is easily disturbed. When the lower leg goes back the rider loses contact with the horse, and is suspended over it. The only contact that remains are the reins. This is unpleasant not only for the rider, but also for the horse.

Rounded back and lowered head are a sure sign that the rider got left behind. The legs often come forward and the seat goes back. In order not to be left behind the rider gets hold of the mane, but in this position he is unable to give the horse's head its freedom, and thereby interferes with it during the jump and on landing.

A rider who is in front of the horse lets his hands go along the mane to the ears. Neck and head reflexes are thereby

B   C

The rider goes with the movements. Three moments in suspension are shown above and below to demonstrate how the rider follows the horse over the jump. The legs are steady against the horse on an imagined plumb-line. The position of the leg against the horse's side and the foot well in the stirrup give the support necessary to leave the upper body free to go forward and come up again. During A and B the rider's body is nearly parallel with the horse's back and neck. In C the upper body comes up a little for the landing. In this way the horse will have least interference. The letters show where the rider is in relation to the jump at the given time.

disturbed as well as the balance, since the rider has lifted his centre of gravity.

While the horse is in the air the rider should try to keep his lower leg straight down, the seat out of the saddle, the upper body bent forward from the hips as far as is necessary to follow the horse's movements. Hands and arms should be in line with the horse's mouth, the head up and looking towards the next jump. Look how economic the rider is with his body and arm movements. Instead of letting his arms go forward even more, he opens his fingers and lengthens the reins without losing contact.

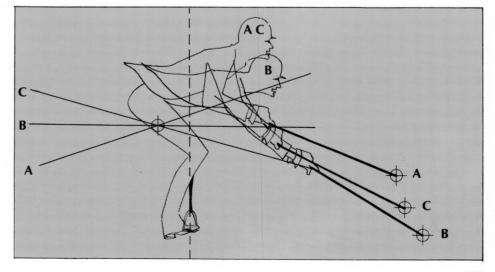

The landing

The fetlock is greatly depressed on landing, as it carries roughly 500 kg weight.

This is the most difficult movement for the horse when jumping. When it is over the jump the front legs are close together and stretched out, but just before touching down they separate and one of them is put down first. The weight on the pastern is about 500 kg or half a ton (*see sketch on right*). The second fore-leg touches down, then the first one is lifted up. The hind-legs, which were pulled up and angled during the jump, are now stretched out and touch down as soon as the second fore-leg is lifted.

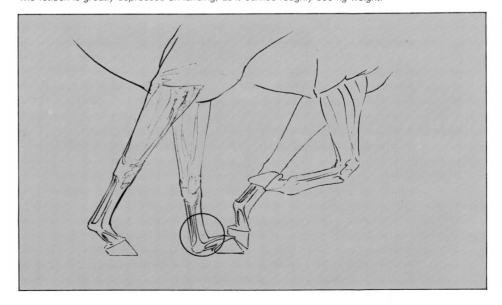

In the moment of landing and in the final canter stride the rider has to follow the horse.

During the first stage of the landing the horse's head is a little pulled in and the neck lifted.

The movement on landing is forward and upward and it is the fore-legs which create this movement. The horse has quickly to make a long flat jump to regain balance.

The rider can help the horse in these movements by sitting light and at the same time giving with hands and arms to enable the horse to stretch its neck at that first canter stride (*see picture above*).

The arching of the horse's back decreases as both the weight and the speed are reduced. Higher jumps and less speed make the landing steeper and put more weight on the hooves and pastern.

To enable the horse to regain balance after the jump it is essential for the rider to go with the movement and to sit as still as possible and not interfere. The first canter stride is determined by the horse's own impulsion. It is only at the second stride that the rider can start to influence the horse without disturbing its rhythm.

When one is jumping combinations, with only one stride in between, these should be treated like 'loose-jumping'. The horse must be given all the freedom it needs to keep its rhythm and balance with a 'passive' rider on top. These combinations are usually more difficult for horses with long strides than for those that have short, active strides. Training can help a lot to teach a horse to shorten its stride, especially working on the collection. It will make jumping much easier for it.

Ignorance and carelessness

These are the greatest enemy of the horse. It is especially in the landing phase that so many horses come to grief. The abnormal increase in weight – about 500 kg on the fetlock when landing from 2m up – can cause all sorts of trouble, especially if there are other difficulties as well. A rider who sits either too far forward or gets left behind has the same effect as a rucksack on a man's back when he jumps over a stream and the rucksack bounces up and down, and this happens at the most difficult moment of the horse's jump. It causes tremendous strain upon the fetlock joints, and can injure them. The ligaments are likely to be pulled and stretched. Ignorance or carelessness can cause the horse to be badly damaged.

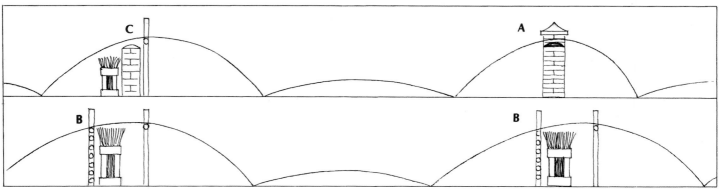

1 *Wall with brush,* **2** *Water. Underneath: 2 doubles (wall with brush),* **C** *Wall with brush,* **A** *Upright wall,* **B** *Oxer,* **B** *Oxer.*

Various fences

There are three types of jump, and they need three different ways of approach to jump them.
Upright — high jumps.
Ditches and water — long jump.
Parallel — high jump.

Uprights

They demand a high jump. The right speed and increased collection are necessary. These jumps (*see picture top left*) are used as first and second jumps in the more novice classes. They must be made to look inviting and easier to jump with the aid of a brush in front of the fence itself. Uprights help horse and rider to jump high, as the shape of the jump makes it easier for the horse to get the angle right (*see upright jump on page 117*).

Spreads — long jumps

These force the horse to jump wide or wide and high.

A water jump is the extreme example of the long jump. The difficulty of a water jump is that it does not give the impression of bulk. A well-built oxer suits the horse much better, as it knows when to take off. The width over an oxer from take-off to landing can be up to ten metres, while a horse finds it difficult to jump a five-metre water-jump. The vision of the horse has also some influence here. An object on the ground which is some way in the distance is only clearly visible to the horse when the light rays meet at a certain angle. (Cf. *page 9*.)

The horse has to come as close as possible to the take-off for the water jump. It must also lift off the ground,

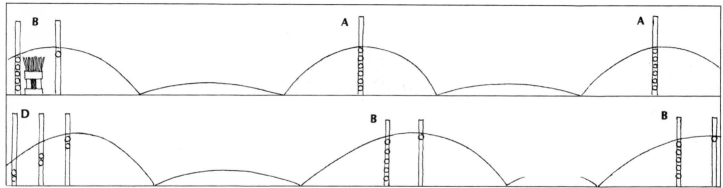

3 *Triple bars,* **4** *Oxer. Underneath: treble,* **B** *Oxer,* **A** *Upright,* **A** *Upright,* **D** *Triple bar,* **B** *Spread,* **B** *Spread.*

though to no great height.

Triple bars demand height and length of a jump and have to be approached at a good speed. The triple bar often asks for great effort by the horse.

Spreads

These demand more of the horse than the previous type of jump, as they differ, and have to be jumped in different ways.

The oxer is a typical spread fence which can be jumped in two ways. The oxer consists of a pole in front and one at the back, with a brush in between. It makes no difference whether the poles are parallel or not, but the thickness and type of in-filling affect the look of the fence and determine how the horse tackles the jump.

At shows

One often encounters obstacles at shows which are completely different to those at home, such as ditches, water jumps and banks, and these can cause problems. Combinations can vary to an amazing degree. The usual combination is uprights, a wall, triple bar and spreads. There can also be included a water jump or ditches with poles over them to make doubles or trebles. The important thing is that there is plenty of room for the combinations and that the distances are correct. The above sketches show some doubles and trebles.

Brushes in front of the wall make it easier for the horse.

High jumps

The jumps shown on these two pages are both high jumps. The height is the same; they are solid and inviting jumps.

The fence on page 116 makes it a lot easier for the horse. There is a brush and some flowers in front of the wall. This helps the horse to find the right place, far enough from the jump, to take off and round itself and really jump well. The fence on page 117 is a straight wall. This is much more difficult for the horse to jump, as it has to find its own ground line for take-off without the help of brush and flowers.

Approach to the high jump

To jump this, the speed can be increased a bit, as the horse will not then get too close for the take-off. Even if the horse takes off a little early it will not matter as it is going faster and has more impulsion and it will manage the jump.

The horse will probably be pulling, but the rider must not stiffen his arms. Instead follow willingly.

Approach to the plain wall

To jump this, the speed should be slightly slower than the ideal speed. The horse has to be well collected for the last few strides. The rider's hands should be passive but retain a strong contact to help the horse shorten its stride and make the strides active. The horse should be able to judge comparatively early when to take off. The great collection should make it possible for the horse to clear the fence, even if it took off too early.

It gets more difficult if the take-off is

A straight wall or upright make it much harder for the horse to find the right place to take off from.

too close to the fence. The horse should have learned to stand off, and in this way shorten the stride. In this situation it can use the 'pole-vault' technique with its fore-legs and the strength in the hind-legs to push up. Horses that do not get too close to the jump seldom take off too early, and usually find the right distance for the take-off.

If the horse gets too close to the jump this usually results in knocking down the pole with the fore-legs, often followed by the hind-legs. The cause of this could easily be that the horse is too keen and the rider cannot control it.

The horse that rushes and does not carry itself

The rider can do the following:

● Allow the horse's nose to go out a little more.

● Sit down lightly in the saddle, with straight legs.

● Lift the hands a little so that the bit presses on the lower jaw, and lengthen the reins a bit.

● Use a martingale to make sure that the bit exerts effective pressure on the bars of the mouth.

Slow it down a lot to begin with, ride the horse quietly forward with a light contact to keep the impulsion going. Sit still in the saddle without making yourself heavy until just before take-off. Give small half-halts all the time until the last stride, when a firm hold on the reins is necessary to help the horse over the jump.

If the horse should stop, growl at it, don't punish it, don't get cross with it, but start again. Click with your tongue and give a bit more with the reins to increase the impulsion.

If the horse just rushes at the jump as soon as it sees it, make several voltes and then ride directly out of the volte to the jump and over it. If the horse still shoots off when facing the jump, halt straight away and repeat this until the horse settles down in the volte and out of it and over the jump. Now slow it down to a halt. Pat it and praise it. Walk on a long rein. This is the way to teach a horse not to rush at a fence but to jump quietly and in balance. After all, it is usually the rider's fault when the horse makes mistakes and misbehaves. Think about that, and practise and practise again.

Rider and horse are in front of the upright. Look at the horse's head, which is up and forward. The lines show the steeper curve of the forehand.

Rustic fences and poles

These should be jumped in the same manner as the wall, though the collection should be increased even more. Poles and especially rustic ones do not give the same solid impression as a wall does. The horses do not respect them as much.

If the horse is really collected it makes no difference if it takes off somewhat too soon or not. This also applies if the speed is reduced.

- Let the horse's nose go out a little more.
- Sit down slightly in the saddle, with straight legs.
- Lift the hands a little so that the bit passes on the lower jaw and lengthen the reins slightly.
- Use a martingale to make sure that the bit applies effective pressure on the bars of the lower jaw.

Slow it down a lot to begin with, ride the horse quietly forward with a light contact to keep the impulsion going. Sit still in the saddle without making yourself heavy until just before take-off. Give small half-halts all the time until the last stride, when a firm hold on the reins is necessary to help the horse over the jump.

If the horse should stop, grumble at it, don't punish it, don't get cross with it, but start again, click with your tongue and give a little more with the reins to increase the impulsion.

If the horse just rushes at the jump as soon as it sees it, make several voltes but not in doubles and especially trebles. For these the speed has to be increased and collection is necessary.

Upright fences are made easier when there is a ground line. It is simpler for a horse to judge the distances when a pole is on the ground, but it is more difficult to jump a rustic where the lowest pole is about half a metre above the ground. The horse does not respect a small, flimsy upright, and frequently knocks it down.

Jumps that have a poor or no ground line must be treated with great respect and good collection. The rider must follow the horse with passive quiet hands, and the movement of the upper body must not influence the hands.

The rider has to wait for the horse to take off, knees well on the saddle, and follow the horse's movements with flexible hands and arms. The rider should be a little behind the horse; 'have the horse in front of the leg' without holding on too much to its head. Be in control of the shoulder and you control the hindquarters and the fetlocks. The horse must be on the bit but in the last canter stride have the nose forward.

Top right: The water jump is the most extreme example of the long jump. Here the rider used the whip to encourage the horse to stretch over the water. Below right is a very difficult jump, as it has the triple bar over the water and the horse has to take off close to get over the pole.

119

Spreads

Water jumps

If the rider could tell the horse to approach the water quite fast and take off at an angle of 50° it would find it quite easy to get over it. The difficulties with water jumps are to make correct use of all the horse's capabilities.

If a small brush is used to make it easier the horse will get off the ground, but if this is taken away the horse sees no reason to jump, and does not do it. The only way to get the horse used to water is to make it familiar with it at an early stage of its training. If this is done it will not be frightened, and will get used to the various speeds at which the rider approaches the different widths of water or ditches.

Start with a small ditch of 1m to 2m and teach the horse to jump over the water. When it has learned to shorten or lengthen its strides the water or ditch can be widened. It is a shame that so few riding schools or clubs have water jumps or ditches over which to train the horses. If the latter had more opportunities to jump ditches and water they would approach them with much more confidence, but one must not become discouraged and force the horse over water. The result could be that it will not go near a water jump again.

Here are some examples of what the rider should do:

Example 1. The rider rides towards a wide ditch. (Only he knows its depth.) He pushes hard but reduces the speed. When the horse has learned not to be frightened of the water it will step into it at the speed asked for. The aids of the rider are clear, and the horse understands them.

Example 2. The rider rides towards a short ditch with water, 2 to 2½ metres long. The speed is increased, and if the horse is unwilling the horseman rides it harder. Just before the take-off he applies pressure with the reins and uses the whip lightly on the shoulder to make the horse take off.

If the horse does not go over the water try next time to tap it with the whip in use (*as shown on page 119*), so that it will make more use of its hind-legs. Also increase the speed. Don't forget to praise the horse even if it does put a foot into the water; it will learn to clear it. The main thing is that it goes near the water or ditch and jumps it.

Triple bar

This should really be jumped like an upright, but the take-off point must be close to the first pole or plank. This the horse has to learn when jumping over different triple bars with the correct distances.

The triple bar is most inviting when it is filled in — or if not filled in, made of planks and not poles, as these give a more solid impression. The American triple bar which consists of two poles for each step gives an even more solid effect. The lowest pole also gives a ground line.

If a triple bar is too bare it can give the impression that the last pole is high, but not as far out as it actually is. If the horse makes a mistake here and takes off too soon without realizing how wide the jump is it can easily have the last pole down.

The speed does not have to be changed if approaching a good solid triple bar, as the horse will jump it well because it looks inviting. If the triple bar is very flimsy, high and wide it is important to increase the speed to some extent and keep the horse well collected during the last few strides. The rider should have the horse 'in front of him' on the bit, and it should have its head up. If it takes off in the right place the angle should be correct in relation to the height of the jump.

If the horse loses speed the result is that it often knocks down the top pole with its hind-legs. The rider must then move it on with the help of the whip. It is important to do it straight after landing. Repeat this several times so that the horse understands that it is better to increase speed before a jump.

When the horse takes off too close to the triple bar (which also happens) it usually results in it pulling down the whole fence. If this was the fault of the horse and not of the rider, pull the horse backward out of the jump, rein back eight or ten steps. Make a quarter-pirouette on the hind-hand and canter on. Canter on a circle which is part of the approach to the jump. Ask for more collection, increase the speed, still keeping the collection. The horse is beginning to understand what is wanted of it, and will find it easier to take off correctly and with more spring in its hind-legs.

Parallels

The oxer (*see pages 87 and 108-9*) is the classical parallel. It is the most difficult type of jump. Two high poles have to be got over, an upright combined with a spread.

Well-filled-in jumps, though high and wide, are inviting, and horses jump them well. A jump that is bare, though lower, can be more difficult to jump. Parallels test the ability of the horse to its utmost. The horse must be collected, it must be really able to get off the ground and bascule. The angle (a little more than 50°), the increased speed and the cor-

A *The horse is first loose-jumped. Put the top pole diagonally from the front to the back. Move the cavalletti back 50cm so that the horse is forced to put in a stride.*
B *With the rider. The back pole is on the back stands; it is slowly moved back and later raised.*

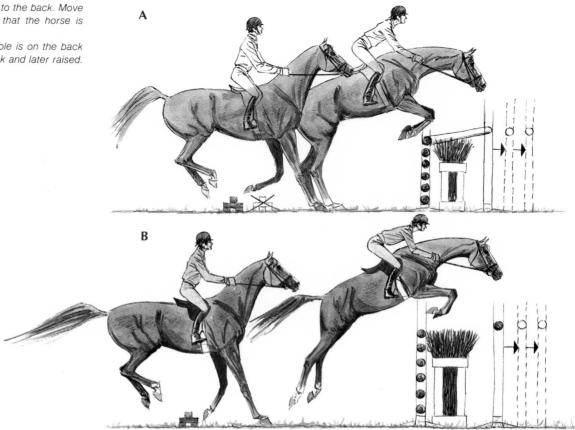

rect take-off combine to create the right conditions for a good jump. The rider who knows what is important to achieve a perfect jump rides with more care than he does in training. Big parallels look intimidating, and one must encourage the horse. There are several ways in which the rider can do this, with the necessary assumption that the horse has had sound jumping training.

A Loose-jump the horse in such a way that it is forced to solve the problem for itself.

B The rider must have studied the horse when it was loose-jumping and learned how it solved the problems and then try to fit in with the horse and follow it.

A. Loose-jumping. Put a cavalletti or a pole about 2·20m in front of the oxer (which is 90 × 90cm), then put the top pole diagonally across from the front to the back. The horse will quite likely attempt to jump it as one fence in-

cluding the cavalletti, and it will knock down the diagonal pole.

Increase the distance of the cavalletti from the oxer by another 50cm. The horse will now be forced to put in a stride between cavalletti and oxer. When the horse clears the oxer the diagonal pole can be put on the far stand. Gradually increase the distances between the front and back poles. First widen the jump, then put it up higher. In this way the horse will learn to respect the jump, and jump it correctly.

B. With the rider Start off with the cavalletti at the distance where the horse has put in a stride between it and the parallel. Eventually take away the cavalletti. Make the fence narrower and lower if the horse finds it difficult and cannot manage it. The practice session must finish on a good note with a good jump.

Spreads

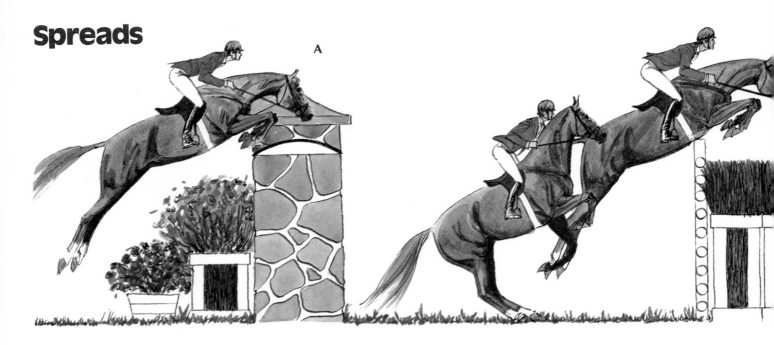

A

Combinations

The distances in between combinations are of the greatest importance (*see table on page 89*). Trebles in this picture have distances of 7·50m to 10·50m. The distance between A and B is 7·50m + 0·20m = 7·70m, while between B and C it is 10·50m + 0·20m = 10·70m.

The combination is rather difficult. The rider will have to give it serious thought. In the first place, how much collection should he ask for? Secondly, how fast to go and what impulsion is needed and the actual outline of the horse. The line of approach is most important, the horse must be straight and be kept straight all the way to the first fence, and the second and third.

This upright **A** assists the horse to find the correct take-off because of its shape (*compare with page 116*). The jump is approached at a fair speed. While the horse is over jump **A**, it sees oxer **B**. The rider has therefore got to keep the horse going with a strong leg and hand.

The horse needs increased collection and energy in the canter to keep the speed and impulsion between the jumps.

When riding through combinations the rider must co-ordinate his movements with those of the horse, and with supple hands give it enough freedom to be able to take off at the right moment. In between the jump the rider, besides

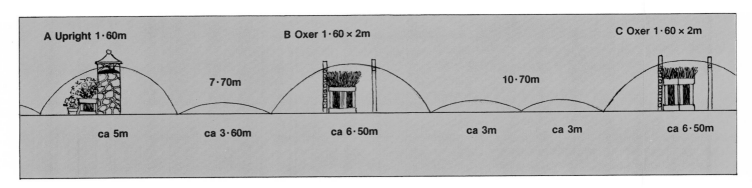

A Upright 1·60m		B Oxer 1·60 × 2m			C Oxer 1·60 × 2m
	7·70m		10·70m		
ca 5m	ca 3·60m	ca 6·50m	ca 3m	ca 3m	ca 6·50m

B   C

*Combination with **A** upright 1·60m **B** Oxer 1·60m × 2m and **C** Oxer 1·60 × 2m. The diagram on p.122 shows the distance and strides between the jumps.*

watching the impulsion, can click with the tongue and if necessary press with his legs. The direction is controlled with the leading rein and corrected if necessary, perhaps supported with weight and legs. The hands must not pull back. A light and soft contact with the bit is right, but it must be firm enough so that the horse knows straight away when the rider gives just before the take-off.

Jump **B**. Oxers must be jumped with all the strength that an increased collection can create. A 3·5m stride after landing over jump **A** should result in a 6·5m jump over the oxer. The horse should come up as soon as landing, but also have time in the air over the jump to pull its hind-legs up and under its body to be able to jump off again. During this stride between jumps the rider can encourage the horse by clicking and using his legs. These small aids are perhaps just what the horse needs to get over the big oxer.

The distance between **B** and **C**, which is the same type of oxer, is greater. The horse has room for two strides after land-ing over jump **B**, as this is a more difficult landing than over jump **A**. The landing after a high parallel is more difficult, as it is steeper, and thereby impedes the rising up again. The rider has to try to help the horse after the first canter stride by not disturbing it at all. Only when the horse takes its second canter stride should the rider push the horse on and over the second oxer.

The rider must on no account lose contact with the horse's mouth over **B**. The legs, supported by clicking, must push the hind-legs forward and under the body. With the help of a passive hand, the horse will be able to take off at the right place to jump fence **C**.

It depends very much on how the horse reacts before and during the combinations as to how the rider will tackle it.

Trebles cannot be practised too often, as they are very demanding, both physically and psychologically. Practice and experience have to be arrived at by loose-jumping and gymnastics. Really big and wide fences should be jumped only occasionally, and not unless the horse is in peak condition and well prepared.

Eventing

Dressage, road and tracks, steeplechase, cross-country, show-jumping. These five are the disciplines asked for at three-day events, and the rider has to be more than competent at each.

1. The rider has to be able to ride dressage up to Medium standard.
2. The rider must be able to jump a B & C course showjumping.
3. The rider must be able to work out the speeds to ride the roads and tracks.
4. The rider must be able to ride over a steeplechase course.
5. The rider must be able to jump cross-country fences at a good speed.

This is not just riding. The rider must really be able to master all these, and to understand them completely, as well as to be able to judge the terrain and use it in such a way to save his horse as much as possible. Training and other preparations must be fully understood.

The most important thing before riding cross-country is to walk the course, not just once but three or four times. Take paper and pencil with you. Try to draw each fence from above, make notes about the state of the ground and undulations. Try to work out the best way to land over the fences: alternatives, which ways are the quickest, which the easiest for the horse. Where to go fast, where to slow down. Discuss the course with the Chef d'équipe or with an experienced friend and compare notes and see whether you are on the right road or not. Go on your own when you are walking the course for the last time. Try and get a clear picture of the whole: the approaches, the jumps, the landings. When you are riding the course it should feel as though you have been over it several times. That is cross-country riding!

The horse at events – a disciplined devil

A good event horse must have the following attributes:
- Strong heart and lungs and a good temperament.
- Really jump well.
- Be disciplined.
- Good stride to cover the ground and great activity.
- Have courage and endurance.

Three-day event – Military – Concours Complet d'Équitation – is the most difficult of competitive riding as it comprises dressage, roads and tracks, steeplechasing, cross-country and show-jumping.

It is necessary not only to have a good horse, but a very good horse; one that is brave, clever and trusts its rider completely.

Dressage test

This is supposed to be a test of obedience of the horse. It is often difficult for the event horse to do a good dressage test, as it has to be extremely fit for the other disciplines. The difficulties caused by the horse are not being used to dressage tests and not obedient enough. The rider should take it early in its career to dressage shows and to ride novice tests. This will help it get used to such events, and will discipline it. The horse soon learns what the dressage saddle, the double bridle and the rider's clothes mean, and will pay attention in the arena. The rider must be relaxed, and not fuss before and during the test, and have a quiet hand to settle the excitable event horse.

Roads and tracks

This is like a 'riding in' in more novice classes. In the three-day event the roads and tracks are divided into two parts with the steeplechase phase in between, and are much more demanding for the horse. The first part is about 6000m long, and the speed is 240m per minute, so that it lasts 25 minutes. The rider has to know how to conserve the strength of the horse so that it is able to cope with the further demands that will be made on it.

Steeplechase

This is usually ridden over a grass track or sand. In the advanced classes it is 3450 to 4140m long, with 12 fences up to 140cm (solid up to 1m) high. Speed 690m per minute. The ideal time is about 6 minutes.

Racing is usually done by Thoroughbreds. The event horse should be about ¾ to ⅞ths Thoroughbred, to have enough stamina to gallop over big fences at speed.

The second roads and tracks

This should be ridden like the first one at a speed of 240m per minute. The distance is about 1200m over roads and tracks, which takes about 50 minutes.

The rider must have the timing worked out all the way. Before starting the cross-country there is a compulsory pause and veterinary inspection. The horse would not be able to start the cross-country if it were exhausted or lame. The time has to be worked out in such a way that the pause is not too long, as the horse would get cold and stiff. Use the pause to the best advantage. Sponge the horse down, and dry it off. Check the bridle and saddle, cool its legs and look at its shoes.

The cross-country

In the advanced classes this is 7980m long, at a speed of 570m per minute. This works out at 14 minutes for the course over 35 jumps in difficult and undulating country. The fences can be up to 140cm high and solid up to 120cm. Long jumps can be up to 4m; spreads may be up to 2m wide at the highest point.

It is an absolute must for the rider to walk the course before riding it – as many times as may be necessary to really get the feel of the fences and the different approaches. The more familiar the rider is with the course, the easier it will be for him to ride it, and use the horse's strength and ability to the best advantage.

The horse must be pulling on to the fences all the time, even when there are fences it has never seen before. Its confidence in the rider must never flag. It takes courage to jump into a lake without knowing its depth, or jump big solid oxers without being able to see the landing on the other side. The rider's hands must encourage all the time, regardless of what the fences look like. The big demanding fences must be jumped with energy and willingness, though the horse may be tiring after going up and down hill, in soft sand or heavy ground which saps its strength. Now the horse has to prove itself, not give up, and draw on its hidden strength to be able to conquer the difficulties. The only thing the rider can do is to take hold of the neck strap and not interfere with the horse. The properly trained and conditioned horse will get its second wind and carry on to such an extent that the rider may have difficulties in stopping it at the end of the course.

Show-jumping

The course is about 800m, speed 400m per minute, height of the jumps about 1·20m and width 2m. This may not sound very impressive, but one must not forget what the horse has done the day before, which was most demanding.

Visibly exhausted horses are not allowed to compete, and no lameness escapes the sharp eye of the veterinary inspector on the morning of the jumping phase. The strain on the legs of the day before shows itself in swelling, especially when standing for some time, and that is why many horses are walked about for hours before the show-jumping. Cooling bandages, cold water, massage — everything is tried to present the horse in the best possible condition for the show-jumping.

Fit, well-trained horses can go very well over difficult cross-country courses, but the horse which has a lot of Thoroughbred in it has great advantages. The Thoroughbred usually has a better gallop, its respiration is better and it develops earlier.

A well-bred pony is tough and hard. The Arab has endurance and toughness, together with an exceptional temperament. A Thoroughbred is fast, has stamina and toughness with an extraordinary will and fighting spirit. The Warm-blood (half-bred) has substance, strong bones, is weight-carrying and accepts discipline and is obedient. The perfect event-horse breeding might look like the diagram opposite.

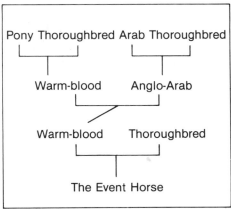

Dressage test

The idea of the dressage test as part of the 'event' is to test the obedience of the horse and its ability to carry out the rider's wishes quietly. The horse must be on the bit the whole time, straight and with plenty of impulsion.

The test ridden in an event is of lower standard than advanced dressage tests, but even so it has to be carefully ridden. It is important to get the best possible points in this first discipline of an event.

As has been pointed out earlier, it can be difficult to ride a dressage test with an event horse that is very fit and near Thoroughbred. It is therefore up to the rider to prepare the horse for the test. The dressage saddle and spurs (but no whip) are pointers for the horse to be quiet. The bitting depends on the F.E.I. rules, and is either snaffle or simple double bridle. No side-reins are permitted.

The rider has therefore the chance to make the horse realize what is being asked of it by putting on the double bridle. This makes it easier to give the required aids. It makes it easier to ride straight, to halt and do pirouettes at the required spot. It must not be used too strongly to discipline the horse. It must not restrict its movements so that it loses the cadence of its steps and impulsion. The ideal, of course, is if the horse can be ridden in an ordinary snaffle.

The training should be directed to the horse being able to do the test with impulsion and rhythm. It should be noticeable how smoothly and forward-going the well-trained event horse does its test.

The event rider feels, of course, that the cross-country is the most important phase, which he looks forward to with great expectation. The dressage seems just a curtain-raiser. No way! Dressage is the elegant side of the competition, where horse and rider are elegantly turned out and move gracefully and elegantly. Here the pair offer themselves to judgment of their movements. The horse's obedience, its attention to the rider and willingness to accept bit and aids, is judged. Here the rider is judged as well, his seat and his proper application of the aids.

Dressage has a psychological effect which must not be neglected. The aim is to build a solid foundation, which takes a lot of patience. A well-schooled horse will find it much easier to cope with difficult and unforeseen situations than another without the training. It has control over its strength. The event horse should be like a devil but one with discipline; it is courageous and has a lot of ability, but is also submissive.

Show-jumping

The difficulty of the show-jumping course is not its height or width. In advanced events there are ten to twelve jumps, maximum height 1·20m and width 2m, and water jump no more than 3m, including a small brush in front of it. The length of the course is 750 to 900m, at a speed of 400m per minute.

This is nothing exceptional for an event horse. The difficulty is to have the horse supple again after it has been over the exacting cross-country course the day before. The terrific strain, both physical and mental, of that course leaves its mark; the horse is usually stiff, and its muscles ache. It has therefore got to be worked slowly and carefully to ease the muscles and make them supple again. This is tedious. The horse resists, and the rider feels sorry for it. It can take more than an hour for the muscles to be warm and soft again. Then the rider has to show the horse that collection is needed to jump these light fences that come down.

It is no good to jump flat and fast or perhaps rush at the fences. The horse has to be made to understand this over the practice jumps. When the horse has been warmed up, is collected and not tense, then the rider can take it into the arena to jump the course. It will then be able to go forward and jump well. It might start to blow after a few jumps; the speed should then be reduced to keep the collection.

Fitness training

See that the horse is relaxed on the long rein. Start trot without asking for collection. Alternate between trot and canter. Slowly increase the degree of balance.

Fitness has to be built up from an early age. A half-bred horse cannot increase its intake of oxygen after the age of 3½ to 4 years.

The basic condition of the event horse has to be started early and built up slowly and sympathetically. This is important so that there will be no damage to the bones, the ligaments, joints and muscles. It is important to have a warm-up period of 20 to 30 minutes before each training session, so that the horse is at the right working temperature. It takes this time for it to be really warmed up and suppled. The temperature has then risen from about 37·5° to 39°. Only at the end of the first work period will the horse go well; the temperature will then have risen to 40°−40·5°. The warming-up period can be divided as follows:

Time in Minutes	Work
00	Walk on a long rein. Turns just with weight and leg-aids.
05	Get hold of the reins, continue in walk. Turns on the forehand and leg-yielding.
10	Trot without collection. Rising trot. Continue trotting, leg-yielding. Volte canter on and ask for more activity.
15	Ask for more balance and activity from behind. Alternate trot and canter.
20/30	More and more is asked of the horse during the last ten minutes. The fitness of the horse has to be built up during this time (*see page 132*).

Gallop work

This must be started with a good foundation and the horse in balance. Start off with a quiet canter about every fifth day. After a few weeks, every fourth day. Twice 5 minutes at a speed of 350m per minute. After a few times this can be increased to 10 minutes. Also slowly increase the speed to 400m per minute. Two periods of canter of 1000m with a few minutes' rest in between. Then three periods of canter of 1000m in 400m per minute.

After about two months the speed can be increased to 500m per minute and three periods of canter of 1000m with rests in between. The lengths of the canter are then increased to 1500m. Try to get the speed up to 490m per minute. This is the speed for a novices' event. Watch your horse carefully during the training.

- Canter over good ground. Loose earth or sand are tiring.
- The horse should canter with the hind-legs well engaged and active ground-covering strides.
- The horse is balanced between legs and hands.
- When the horse is doing fast work it should never be up to its limit and always able to go faster.
- The horse must not get tired.

Interval training — up and down hills, which puts more pressure on the horse's muscles than anything else, and strengthens them.

The rider has to learn to recognize the correct speed and how to keep it. Ride a certain distance in the time required. A wristwatch or chronometer is essential for this.

The easing off after the work is as important as was the warming-up period. Keep the horse moving in walk until heart and lungs work normally again. Lead it as long as it is sweating. Take care of it.

The horse should carry itself in the canter and be balanced between leg and hand.
Below: In the fast work, ride only so fast that it is still possible to go faster. The rider has to recognize the right speed and keep to it.

Work to build up the horse

This has to be carried on all the time. The ligaments, joints and tendons have to be straightened so that they can withstand the strain. This work should be fitted into the programme three times a week. To begin with spend 4-5 minutes in trot over different types of country and different going. Trot for 10 minutes, rising — at a medium speed, if possible — in woods, gravel paths, over logs, fields etc. The horse should be on the bit all the time and react quickly to the rider's aids, as well as looking where it is going. The work must never be monotonous or boring. The co-ordination between horse and rider has to be practised so that they approach the various problems together. The trot period is interchanged with a walk period. The walk is on a long rein, with light leg-contact. Horses like going along the beach. Trotting in knee-deep water strengthens the legs and at the same time cools the tendons.

Start with 10 minutes trot alternating with 10 minutes walk (altogether 40 to 50 minutes), increasing it to reach 90 minutes in about 6 weeks. This work is designed to strengthen the horse so that it will be able to go over long distances and uneven ground, including the jumps, without tiring.

Timing

This is extremely important for the road tracks, the steeplechasing and cross-country. The time taken can play a deciding role in events, so the rider has to learn the art of riding to the clock. The feel of the speed must be practised and practised again until the rider is quite sure how fast 240m/minute, 690m/minute and 570m/minute are.

There are many methods for learning this. Measure 240m on different paths and tracks on which you ride fast work, then try to ride each one in exactly one minute. Take a track of 1000m and ride that in 10 minutes, partly in trot, partly leading the horse, partly in canter, while keeping an eye on the watch. Then try to remember what the speed felt like when you were trotting, leading the horse and cantering. The rider should be able to repeat this exercise without hesitation and without having to look at his watch

(*for the speed on the racecourse see page 135*).

The rider has to vary the speed, when riding cross-country, according to the conditions of the ground, the fences and the inclines. A distance of 1000m can contain all sorts of variations: a jump in and out of rails, a climb down to and over a ditch with post and rails, a ride in a thick wood, a windy stony path, followed by a drop of 2m. Then through a quarry, then a jump into water, a jump in the water and over an obstacle and out of the water, then a climb up a steep hill. A thousand metres should be ridden in a little under two minutes. No wise event rider rides such a section at a speed of 570m/minute, as the difficulties are too great — stony path drop fence — very short canter, perhaps trot. In the quarry, perhaps slide down. Water jump, relatively slowly into the water, other-

wise there is the danger of stumbling, as the water at a depth of 70cm acts as a brake. Jump out of the water, no possibility to increase the speed. Straight after that a climb up to 45°, 30m difference in height.

The part of the course just described slows the speed down a lot. The rider must be able to judge how much time he needs for each section and where he can find the best going. Here one has to think and be able to calculate the time and work out the best way of riding. It is impossible to give advice that applies to everything. Each rider has to learn to judge through experience, whether in the novice classes or in the very advanced ones. Some riders just have a feel for it. Many never learn to evaluate the horse's ability to perform the tasks that are asked of it.

Roads and tracks

Horses have sometimes had to cover incredibly long distances. The White Russian leader Count Wrangel gave a graphic description of all that the 1920 retreat from the Ukraine entailed. In the middle of winter, with very low temperatures, the cavalry covered 1400km in 75 days, through country that was devastated by years of war, without sufficient food and with almost daily fighting. On some days they were unable to move on because of the fighting. The retreat was done in stages also at night, sometimes covering as much as 40km at a time. On the last days (from 16 to 20 February) they covered 280km, with 100km of these on 19/20 February with only 4 hours rest at night.

Four things made it possible for the horses to withstand the rigours of the trek:
1. Their good basic condition, improved with steady and progressive work.
2. There was always a blacksmith available, with a store of shoes and nails. The lost shoes were always collected.
3. The equipment was kept in as good a condition as possible, and numnahs and saddle cloths had to be soft.
4. The grooms were well-trained and well-equipped. The farriers had some veterinary knowledge, and could cope with simple injuries.

It might be mentioned that the Austrian cavalry was virtually unable to fight right from the beginning of the First World War, as their saddles were too hard. Event riders should note:

● Choose a suitable horse and carefully improve the fitness.
● Make certain it is well shod.
● Look after the saddlery and make sure it is in good condition.
● Be consistent with the horse's training.

On the steeplechase course

At events a horse goes singly over the steeplechase course, so it is not a race in the proper sense. Most event riders do not have the opportunity to train on a racecourse, where the going is generally good. The speed at three-day events is 690 metres per minute, which demands a good foundation training.

Like all other phases of eventing, this one has to be trained for. It is not just a question of the jumps, or the speed, but of jumps and speed together. A distance of 4140 metres in 690 minutes is asking a lot, and sufficient opportunity for suitable training has to be given. The best has to be made of any available facilities. A nice big field or a long path in the woods is sufficient. With a little imagination one or two jumps can be transformed into five or six, or uprights can be used as a basis.

The speed of the steeplechase course is considerable, and the horse must be willing to go on. It is ideal if it pulls on enough, so that it does not have to be pushed. The rider can then regulate the speed with a low passive hand and flexible seat. The length of the stirrups is up to the rider. It is preferable to have them fairly short, in order not to interfere with the movement of the horse's back.

The jumps are very long over the fences at speed, and the horse brushes through the top of them. However, horses soon learn how much they can brush through before hitting the solid part of the jump. The steeplechase phase has to be ridden in complete harmony between horse and rider. If the rider is not firm in the saddle it can be compared with a puncture in a car at high speed.

Cross-country

For most event riders the cross-country phase is the one that really matters and appeals. Here is the proof of the pudding as to the horse's ability, its courage and obedience and willingness as well as fitness; they are all put to the test.

Here the rider too knows his prowess and courage and his ability to assess the course correctly, which is the most difficult thing to do. The training for the cross-country phase must therefore be as varied as possible. It can be difficult for the rider to find suitable terrain near by, so he has to try to make the best of what he has. Build the fences in such a way that they can be jumped from both sides, and group them together in combinations. Build them so that the height and width can be changed. It is not too difficult to build a water jump. A bit of plastic sheeting, five spades and twenty youngsters can work wonders! All sorts of other fences can be built with a little imagination and energy to create varied training facilities.

Cross-country training

The look of the fences and their position can make great demands on the horse's suppleness and technique. Before starting any cross-country section the horse must be carefully warmed up and suppled. Do not train it over too high fences if it is not necessary. If a horse has the ability to jump big fences, there is no need to school it over them, as it only puts unnecessary pressure on it and can take away the pleasure of jumping. Concentrate on the things that the horse

cannot do as well.

It is most important to practise the approaches, so that the horse can jump off a short stride where necessary. It should 'slide down' the other side so that it will not lose its balance on landing. When the horse rushes at a fence this can be because it is used to going faster over open country. The rider must make a rule not to go faster as soon as he is in open country. Make sure to vary the cross-country training. If the horse is allowed to increase speed over open country it must be brought back to trot or walk the next time. The event horse has to be obedient.

Really difficult obstacles can worry a rider sometimes, although he should know how the horse will react to it, how it should be ridden and perhaps corrected. Horses often like to rush at a fence, and this can be the fault of the rider who when the obstacle is in sight unconsciously changes his weight and aids and moves his head. The rider turns, and turns the horse too early with him. The horse must be ridden forward until it is turned with the correct aids. The horse should not anticipate where the rider wants to go, but wait for the aids.

It could make some difference whether the rider is right- or left-handed. This is specially noticeable in combinations where the horse looks to the left (the right, if the rider is left-handed). The horse jumps the first fence in the middle, the second to the left and runs out to the left at the third. This is caused by the rider not having much feeling in his left hand and therefore not using his right hand properly and losing contact.

Cross-country fences

Just as in show-jumping, fences consist of uprights, spreads, water jumps and ditches. Added to these are jumps in and out of water, banks and dykes. The big difference is that cross-country fences are fixed, whatever impression they might give to the contrary. The following pages show how these obstacles — which vary from the show-jumping ones — should be ridden.

Typical cross-country fences

Banks and dykes of all types and proportions should be present at all cross-country courses (*see picture above*). These jumps should be approached at a fair speed. The post and rails at the take-off side are fairly steep in front of the bank, and the one on the right makes the landing easier for the horse. A slight hesitation before jumping off helps it to more or less glide over the second post and rails. If the horse hesitates in the middle of the jump the rider must use a strong leg and give with his hands.

The road (*below*) lies between two banks. This has to be approached slowly for the last few strides, preferably in trot so that the horse can find a suitable spot for take-off and for landing between the two posts and rails, leaving itself enough room for take-off again. The stride between the two posts and rails should be short and collected so that the horse has every chance to get over the second post and rails. The rider must make certain that he goes with the horse on landing so as to be able to push it on to get the necessary impulsion. It might be necessary to hold on to the neck strap.

The bank (*above*) This has a wall on the top of it. This obstacle needs careful thinking by the rider. The horse considers this a nice jump, and often jumps it with true bascule (rounding of back). The approach should not be too fast, so that the horse can use itself properly and jump calmly over the wall. If it is going too fast and rushes at it, it could easily slip on landing after the wall if the going is at all slippery. The rider must follow the movements of the horse and give with his arms and hands so that it can really use itself. The horse then has the chance to be collected again.

Steps (*below*). These are ridden at a medium speed. The horse must not be allowed to land too far forward on the first step, as it would have to jump the second from a standstill. It cannot use its hind-legs properly from this position and is forced to lift itself from an almost sitting position, which needs a great deal of energy. When properly approached, the horse should be able to put in one short stride. This enables it to have enough impulsion for the second step. In this way the effort is distributed over all four legs equally. If the steps are built as an 'in and out' the rider could perhaps jump it at a slant, so that the horse can put in a stride and save energy.

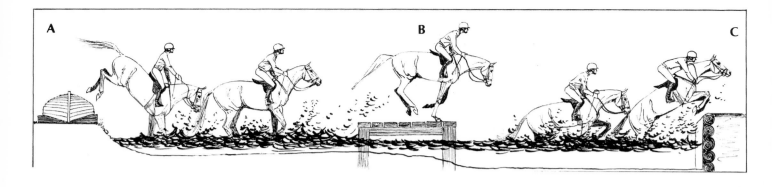

Water jumps

These should not create difficulties if the horse is schooled properly. 'The Harbour' above is a well-constructed obstacle with the upturned boat at **A**, footbridge at **B** and an embankment at **C**. This should not be too difficult for a brave event horse and a thinking rider. The rider should ride slowly and quietly with collection towards the boat, which might frighten the horse. Keep your legs well on, click, keep hold of the reins to keep the horse straight. If the water is deeper than 30 to 40cm the horse should slip into it. If it is 70 to 80cm deep the water resistance is very great, and forces the horse to either wade or make big jumps. With the reins in one hand and the other on the neck strap the rider must try to stay with the horse all the way in and out of the water. It makes it much easier for the horse if the water is shallow, 30 to 40cm. How the horse jumps off the landing-stage depends on the depth of the water. If it is more than 80cm the horse has to wade. The jump out of the water has to be made almost from a standstill, which makes it very difficult for the rider to follow the horse's movements.

The coffin

This is a relatively difficult jump combination which tests the horse's courage (*see below*). When approaching the first element of the jump **A**, the ditch must look very intimidating to the horse, and it should therefore have good collection, be well between leg and hand and be ridden at **A** with short canter strides. When getting close to **A** the rider should encourage the horse with clicking and make it feel his own determination. **A** should be jumped with a short jump so that it does not slide too close to the ditch. Having got over **A**, the ditch does not look so frightening any more, and **B** should not complicate matters. Jump **C** can be considered easy.

The most important thing when schooling the horse to jump coffins is to convince it that the jump is not as dangerous as it looks. This really applies to most of the complicated cross-country fences.

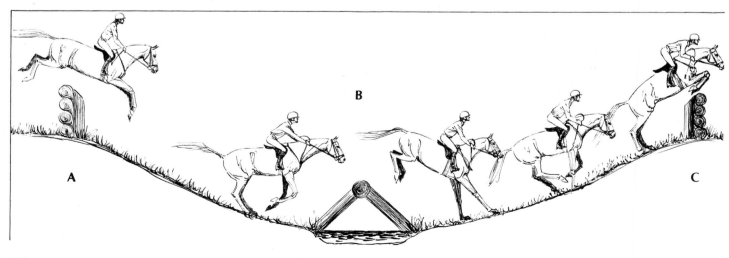

Big spreads into water

These really test the horse's confidence in the rider (*above*). If the horse could not see the water behind the jump there would be no problem, but here it sees the water, and does not know the depth. The jump is too big to clear, and the horse has to land at some speed. It all depends on the experience the horse has had with water jumps. If it has gained confidence in the rider during the training periods, if it is mentally and physically adjusted and has not had any unpleasant experiences, this jump should cause no problems. The approach should be at speed so that the horse can clear the fence and land well out in the water. The water for these types of jump must not be too deep, as this reduces the danger of the horse stumbling on landing.

Ditches

These sometimes create a psychological difficulty for the rider, while a well-trained horse generally approaches them without hesitation, even when they are big, and have a tiger trap etc., over them. It is important for the rider to ride strongly at them and then let the horse take over.

The Ditch (*below*). This ditch should be approached slowly, perhaps even in trot, so that the horse can get close to the fence to take off and land not too far out the other side, as landing on the steep slope would put great strain on its ligaments and tendons. A ditch of 2 to 3m with a similar fence over it, but on level ground, would be jumped and approached at a great speed.

Index

ABILITIES OF THE HORSE   14
Accompanying the horse   21
Aids of the rider   27
Approach:
   to the upright   116
   to the wall   116-17
Arab   127

BACK MUSCLES OF HORSE   40
Balance of the horse   8, 40, 84, 91, 98
Balance reflexes of the horse   10
Basic riding instruction   26-8
Bits   13, 21, 47, 82
Breast-plate   82
Breeding   14
Brush   89

CANTER   34, 40, 54-9
   as a pace   54
   collected   55
   counter-   34, 55, 56
   extended   55
   flying changes   54, 56-9
   four-time changes   59
   in four-time   34, 54, 93
   in three-time   34, 92
   medium   34
   one-time changes   59
   shortened   34
   three-time changes   59
   training for events   131
   with increased collection   92
Cavalletti   22, 86, 121
   work   20, 22, 40, 88
Cavesson   21
Central nervous system of horse   8, 10
Chambon   22, 83

Circles   60, 61
Clicking   27
Coffin   140
Collection   48, 91-2
Corners, riding through   27
Crooked horse   28, 38-9
Cross-country   126, 136-41
   fences   137
   jumping   115, 126
   riding   124
   training   136-7

DITCHES   114, 120, 141
Double:
   bridle   47, 128
   reins   26
Draw-reins   23, 83
Dressage   10, 40, 46-77, 91
   horse   46, 47
   saddle   47
   seat   26
   shows   48
   test   126
   test (eventing)   128
Driving   21, 40, 90

ELEVATION   108
Equipment:
   dressage horse   47
   show-jumper   82
Eventing   124-41
Events   126
   horse   127
Exercises in lateral work   66

FENCES   118, 138
Fetlock (landing)   112
Fitness training   90, 130
Flexion of hocks   62

Flying changes   54, 56-9
Foals   16, 19
Footfalls:
   in canter   34
   in dressage   48

GATE   89
Gogue   83
Ground conditions   12
Growing pains   20
Growing process   20
Gymnastic jumping   89

HACKING   25
Half-bred   21, 127
Half-halt   28, 31, 34, 41, 42, 53, 60, 68
   on the forehand   98
Half-pass   62, 65
Half-pirouette   57, 61, 62
Halt   36, 42-3
Head-collar   18
Hearing of the horse   8
Hind-hand   40
Holding of reins   25, 26, 27
Hoof   12-13
Horse:
   crooked   28
   green   24, 40
   straight   38
   trained   40
   two-year-old   20-1
   yearling   20
   young   24

INHERITED CHARACTERISTICS   14

JOGGING   32
Jump:

combinations 87, 88, 122-3
training 20
Jumping:
  cross-country 115, 126
  lanes 86
  saddle 82
See also Show-jumper,
  Show-jumping
Jumps 114-20
  approach 94
  over the 96

LAMENESS 13
Landing 96
Leg-yielding 30, 64-5
Levade 73, 84
Lipizzaners 85
Loin muscles 25
Loops 60
Loose-jumping 86-7, 121
Lower jaw 28
Lunge whip 21
Lungeing 20, 21, 22

MARTINGALE 83
Medium:
  trot 50
  walk 48
Muscles of the horse 6
Muscling up 9

OVERREACH BOOTS 82
Oxers 89, 115, 120, 121, 123

PACING:
  trot 33
  walk 32
Pain 13
Parallels and spreads 114-15,
  120-1

Passage 46, 65, 72, 76
Piaffe 46, 61, 72, 76
Pillars 74
Pirouette 61
  half- 57, 61, 62, 65, 68, 91
Practice jumps 36

RACING TROT 25, 33, 36, 53
Reflexes of the horse 8, 10, 18
Rein-back 37
Reins 23, 26, 32, 87
Renvers 64, 91
Rising trot 25, 33, 36, 53
Roads and tracks 126, 134

SADDLE 8, 13, 21, 24, 47
  sores 13
Salute 43
Seat of the rider 53
  rising 26, 81, 99, 102
  upright 81, 99, 102
Senses of the horse 8-9
Shoes 12
Shoulder-in 64, 66, 68
Show-jumper 80
  equipment 82
  technique 84
Show-jumping 115, 129
Side-reins 83
Sideways movement 30
Sitting 24
  trot 33
Skeleton of the horse 7
Skin of the horse 8
Snaffle 21, 31
  bit 21, 47
Speed training (eventing) 133
Spurs 27
Standing up in the stirrups 33
Steeplechase speed 135

Steps 139
Stirrup leather 26, 89
  buckle 47
Straight horse 38
Straightening of the horse 38
Strides before take-off 94, 98,
  102
Strike-off:
  from trot 54
  in canter 34, 35
Surcingle 82
Suspension:
  in canter 34
  over fence 96, 110

TAKE-OFF 96
  point of 94, 96, 104, 106
Thoroughbred 127
Tilting 11, 107
Touch impulses 8
Transitions:
  from canter to trot 36, 54
  from canter to walk 54
  from shoulder-in to
    travers 70
  from travers to
    shoulder-in 70
  from trot to walk 36
  from walk to canter 54
  from walk to halt 36
  training 70
Travers 64, 68, 91
Trebles 122
Triple bar 89, 114, 115,
  120
Trot 32-3, 36, 50
  collected 50, 76
  extended 50
  false 33, 50
  working 50

Turns:
  on the fore-hand 30
  on the hind-hand 61

VOLTE 28, 57, 61, 62, 65, 68

WALK 32
  as a pace 48
  collected 48
  dressage 48
  extended 48
  false 48
  on a long rein 32, 48
Wall 89
Water:
  ditches 114, 118, 120
  jumps 140
Weight of the rider 12
Whip 27, 30

YEARLING 20

ZIG-ZAG 71